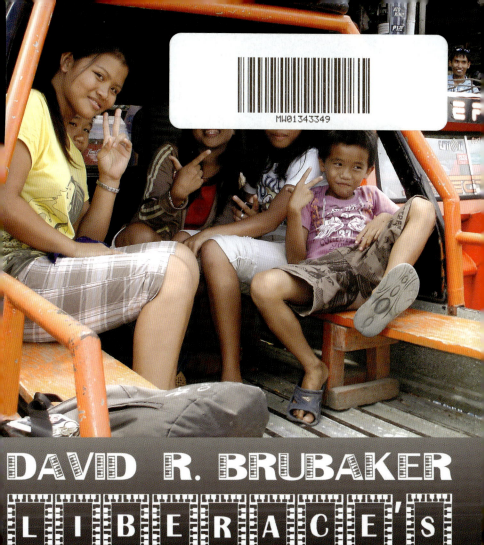

DAVID R. BRUBAKER
LIBERACE's
FILIPINO COUSIN

Liberace's Filipino Cousin
David R. Brubaker

Copyright©2016 ThingsAsian Press

All rights reserved under international copyright conventions. No part of the contents of this book may be reproduced or utilized in any form or by any means, electronic or mechanical, including photocopying and recording, or by any information storage and retrieval system, without the written consent of the publisher.

Front cover font: Liberace by pearlygate
Photos by David R. Brubaker

ThingsAsian Press
San Francisco, California, USA
www.thingsasianpress.com

Printed in Hong Kong

ISBN-10: 1-934159-65-4
ISBN-13: 978-1-934159-65-1

Acknowledgments

I learned long ago to surround myself with the smartest people, folks who could help me overcome my limitations. My deepest appreciation to Kevin Oderman for his guidance and wise counsel in preparing this manuscript, for his unrelenting optimism, high expectations, and teaching me how to craft individual essays and fit them together into a congruent whole. I learned tremendously from him.

There have been several teachers from whom I have learned much, and who have encouraged me to write: Robert Olmstead, Ralph Jenkins, Becky Bradway and David Poyer.

I thank my wife, Marilyn, for her patience and assistance with the manuscript, and for helping me with some of my memories and blind spots. Her close reading of this volume and her devil's advocacy helped enormously. I thank Andrew, Kristen, Roman and Adriane for their tolerance and willingness to reveal themselves.

I am grateful to Albert Wen for making this book a reality. Janet Brown masterfully edited this manuscript and has been an active supporter of Liberace's Filipino Cousin from the beginning. Her diligence, expertise and good humor strengthened the manuscript without changing its basic nature.

Sheri Quirt, with her sharp eyes, improved the manuscript and helped me to significantly reduce the number of errors it contained.

I am especially grateful to the many Filipinos who generously shared their opinions and life stories with me.

Some names have been changed to protect the privacy of individuals.

Contents

7	Prologue	79	Tony
13	Dancing with the Tampon Queen	91	Lucky Buggers
23	Fungus in Paradise	101	All-Arounders
35	Adriane in Ternate	119	Joseph
47	A Good Meal	127	Shakey's
49	Rockwell	131	Evening in Ermita
55	Bolo-Bolo	139	Joy
69	Morning in Makati	145	Epilogue
75	Santo Niño	157	About the Author

Prologue

I've been traveling to the Philippines for more than twenty years. At first I went to visit my son, a Peace Corps volunteer, in a small village in Cavite Province. I didn't know what to make of the Philippines then, and did not foresee that I would soon become enamored of its culture and its history. I visited Andrew several times during his tour and gradually became fascinated by a place so complex, so different, that I wanted to explore all its seven thousand islands. I needed to understand the logic of life there, which I began to think was in some ways superior to our own in the United States. People seemed to enjoy themselves living on the edge, finding creative ways to cope with life in the extreme. Joy amidst destitution.

Later I returned to explore the country on vacation, especially its beaches. When I had a chance to work for the World Bank on a project monitoring the water quality of the Pasig River, which cuts through Metro Manila, I jumped at it. I visited periodically to work with businesses and universities seeking to improve the environment. Lately, I've come to the Philippines to visit my son once again, who is now a resident of the city. As an employee of the Asian Development Bank, his circumstances have changed dramatically from his Peace Corps days.

The essays that follow represent my attempt to understand the Philippines and the lessons that country might offer.

Sometimes I'm asked by a visitor about how best to experience Manila. Where to start? My inevitable answer is: Intramuros.

It reeks of melancholy, sunshine, and macabre beauty. I am drawn here as to no other place, although my family can't understand why and I often visit alone. It's possible to see the story of the Philippines here, to confront your humanity. It is pleasantly uncomfortable, both mentally and physically, in the midday heat. The locals seem oblivious to the bullet holes and the ruins and to the history of the country that can be discerned by walking just a few blocks.

In the ruins of Fort Santiago, I can feel the history—a history of domination, a history of subjugation and violence. Yet life carries on. The ruins are filled with Spanish and American architectural reminders and cheap modern Philippine construction; its ancient streets are cluttered with debris, cars, tricycles, and people; and I begin to wave off the inquiries of passersby. It's hard not to grow irritated by the unrelenting solicitations, many from people up to no good.

The Spanish claimed Intramuros in the sixteenth century and built a walled fort there at the mouth of the Pasig River to keep out intruders. Soon it evolved into a protected enclave, complete with churches, homes, and colleges: a small city-within-a-city, built of stone. Under Spanish rule, which lasted until 1898, there were earthquakes and the occasional foreign incursion. Then the Americans arrived, and the Philippines became a Commonwealth of the United States after the Spanish-American War. The Yankees tried to remake the place, celebrating and promoting Filipino heroes who reflected American values.

The martyred José Rizal, though ethnically Chinese and a Mason to boot, was lionized by the new colonists. Rizal had been executed for subversion by the Spanish in 1896 for agitating for Filipino freedom and for founding *La Liga Filipina*, which was organized to oppose not only the Spanish, but also the wealthy clerical orders. He wrote *Noli Me Tangere*, an indictment of corruption, and *La Solidaridad*, a novel about failed revolutionaries. Rizal was not only a national hero: he fit the American vision of the future of the Philippines. He advocated gradual, nonviolent change, and he was a multiethnic thinker, an internationalist who had traveled widely. He spoke ten languages and was an acclaimed ophthalmologist. He was a reasonable, principled, educated man, the perfect national icon.

The site of his execution in Intramuros is now a garden. A Rizal monument and museum overlook the Pasig River, housed in a restored barrack, and it is peaceful there. You can walk uninterrupted. You can think. Rizal Park, Manila's largest, lies just beyond Intramuros, off Rizal Boulevard.

Lacking funds, for many years the Philippine government did little to protect or restore what remained of the old walled city. During World War II, Intramuros was occupied by the Japanese until they were driven out, killed mostly, by the American and Commonwealth armies. The Americans shelled Intramuros during the Japanese occupation and much of it was destroyed. It was not until after the war that the Philippines became an independent country, ending centuries of domination—at least by foreign powers. Intramuros has evolved into a place to honor heroes. There is a presidential statue garden, eulogizing the nation's presidents, most of whom served prison terms. The garden needs weeding.

The museum and its gardens were the centerpiece of efforts to restore and honor Intramuros, but these efforts stalled long ago. Beyond the Rizal shrine, there hasn't been much upkeep until recently, when shops and guard stations have been built. Statues honoring Spanish kings, Queen Isabella II, and many others were installed by partisans in Intramuros. The *Memorare* recognizes the one hundred thousand people killed during the Battle of Manila.

Now there are tours and vendors. There are souvenir shops where old Japanese banknotes from the occupation are for sale, along with vintage maps depicting what used to be in Manila. Images of the Buddha and Santo Niño, books by and about José Rizal, are all for sale. A lone Starbucks, usually almost empty, serves coffee and quiet. Jollibee, the Filipino version of McDonald's, has a place here, but, so far, there is little other development and few stores with familiar names.

This city-within-a-city now has over five thousand inhabitants. Mixed in among the ruins are nondescript government buildings, some commercial development, and a host of poor people living in shanties. There are few functional sidewalks in Intramuros, and it is easy to trip and fall, as I have done more than once. If I carelessly look skyward while walking, I'm apt to step into a hole or trip over an errant brick.

Walking around Intramuros, I see old buildings like the San Augustin Church, which was constructed in 1607. The façade of this building is badly damaged, and looking closely, I see where shells and bullets have killed people. Nowadays, the church seems to sustain itself with parking fees and charges for special occasions, particularly weddings. I continue walking, past the Governor's Palace, an ugly government building built on the ruins of the original—which was destroyed by an earthquake—and remnants of the old fort, its deteriorated walls damaged by foreign armies fighting for possession of the city, the country.

As I navigate the streets of this cat-infested neighborhood, I see people going about their business, selling, hustling, seemingly oblivious to their surroundings and to the terror that Intramuros has witnessed. Lots of folks are just milling around or sitting in the shade. Oversized straw hats sold by vendors are ubiquitous, as are tricycle drivers, panhandlers, and swindlers of all sorts. The shells of once-grand colonial structures have become monuments to human savagery. The tourists are most interested in finding food and a horse-drawn carriage, in getting their picture taken beside a monument. They suffer in the heat and most don't linger: it's a good place to *have* visited.

On my most recent trip, I returned to the Rizal Shrine to contemplate the risks taken by Filipino patriots more than a hundred years ago, fighting a hopeless battle against an entrenched colonial power. Where are their successors? I wondered what these men would think of the present state of affairs. Would they agitate for a domestic revolution?

As I left the shrine's garden, it began to rain and I sought refuge in a coffee shop around the corner, taking my purchase to the protected patio. The rain turned into a torrential downpour, and I watched a near-toothless woman across the street pull a tarp over the chicken-on-a-stick and *buko* juice, which is water from young coconuts, at her small food stand. She smiled and waved to me. Later, when the rain stopped, I decided to explore what was for me the unfamiliar underbelly of Intramuros. After purchasing a Coke Light from the old woman, I began to investigate flooded streets, where scores of small children played in the runoff. Fighting cocks, tied to lampposts, ignored their owners, hovering nearby. Boys played basketball in the ruins, and I noticed that the Los Angeles Lakers were popular here, at least judging from an informal survey of T-shirts. Lots of folks just hung out, hoping to keep dry and perhaps earn a few pesos hustling visitors or selling wood carvings or postcards to the occasional tourist. Some offered to show me around.

There are several small colleges in Intramuros, which gives the neighborhood a youthful vibe. I was surprised that the guards at the Colegio de San Juan de Letran permitted me to enter the campus and browse at the bookstore. I was looking for books about Philippine history but found few. What I saw were textbooks of a practical nature, books about business, nursing, education, and engineering. The college reminded me of Chinese universities, often housed in overcrowded buildings, with diligent and well kempt students. The School of Liberal Arts at Colegio de San Juan included majors like journalism, legal management, and food technology, rather than fields like philosophy or English.

This struck me as odd, here in Intramuros, surrounded by history. Of course, most countries governed by despots discourage the study of the liberal arts, generally citing economic concerns. The liberal arts are seen both as a threat and an unaffordable luxury. Students majoring in political science or history might become agitators, politically problematic, and unlikely to contribute to the general welfare.

Like the rest of Manila, Intramuros has a faint American feel. You see advertisements for American films and a bookstore filled mostly with volumes from the United States. Yet the colonial architecture, the religion, are vestiges of centuries of Spanish rule. Even the poorest people here speak English, a result of the American occupation. Intramuros could be anywhere in Manila, people surviving in the chaos and decimation, oblivious to their history, disinterested in the past and the meaning of the place. I understand their attitudes. If I grew up here, had their frame of reference, I'd probably feel the same.

I'll be back in Manila in a couple of months, and I'll return to Intramuros. The place suggests unanswerable questions about humanity. It is, somehow, depressing, but at the same time exhilarating. I'll probably go to the Starbucks, too.

Dancing With The Tampon Queen

Barbara, a friend of mine and a professor of organizational strategy at the University of Pennsylvania, asked me about my upcoming trip to Manila. "Promise me you'll look up a former student of mine. She's a senior executive at Consumer Tech, and I think you'll like her." She gave me Charlotte's number and I promised to call. "Good, I'll let her know you'll be contacting her."

"Hello, Charlotte? This is David Brubaker. I'm a friend of Barbara…"

"Yes, David! I've been expecting your call. Barbara told me all about you. I'll send a car for you. About three o'clock? Where are you?"

"The Royal Palm in Ermita. Mabini and Padre Faura."

"Rudolpho will pick you up. I'll show you around Consumer Tech and you can meet the president. Then we'll come to my house for dinner, and later we'll go to the Intercontinental Hotel for a surprise. You're going to have fun!"

I was impressed. This lady was hyperorganized. I put on my *barong*, a lightweight embroidered shirt that is worn untucked, and waited outside for the car, while chatting with Poco, the scruffy doorman outfitted in a bright green, ill-fitting uniform and a comically large hat topped by a gold medallion. A dark Mercedes-Benz limousine with blacked-out windows pulled up to the curb. Immaculately attired in what looked like a handmade blue suit, Rudolpho emerged from the car. "Dr. Brubaker," he said, opening the back passenger door. Poco was impressed, I could tell. Of course, this scene was theater and we all played our roles.

Rudolpho clearly knew how to navigate the clogged Manila streets, taking shortcuts through obscure neighborhoods, driving aggressively but with precision. Street kids banged on the windows, begging for coins, but I didn't have time to react. Rudolpho was that good.

A half hour later we entered the heavily guarded, nondescript Asian corporate headquarters of Consumer Tech. Charlotte was there to greet me. A small American woman in her fifties, with tailored short hair and dressed in corporate attire, she flashed a ready smile. She had a friendly, take-charge demeanor, and she struck me as a person at ease with wielding power. We entered her large office, its size befitting her senior status in the corporation.

But I felt like a character in a *Saturday Night Live* skit. While one table held dozens of tiny bottles of shampoo and conditioner, small packages of tampons were piled on chairs and tables and her desk looked as though it was a tampon shrine. It reminded me of the small Buddhist altars found on street corners throughout Asia. The walls were covered with posters from around the world advertising tampons in all their diversity. Who knew?

Caressing a miniscule bottle of shampoo, I inquired if she stayed at lots of hotels. "You know," she said, "poor people in Asia can't afford full-sized bottles of these products. But the small sizes are often within their reach. We get to introduce consumers to our brand, our products, and we still make money. It's a win-win."

"Tampons must be big movers," I said.

"David, tampons are my specialty, my baby. I'm in charge

of tampon sales throughout Asia, and it's been an unexpected success. You know more than once I've been called the Tampon Queen, and for good reason. We sell more tampons here in Asia than anyone else," Charlotte said proudly, without a bit of irony.

Once again, profit from poverty. Yes, of course they were targeting the growing middle class in places like China and the Philippines, but they were also building brand identity and loyalty in the masses. In Asia, such products are aspirational, coveted as signifiers of upward mobility. The company was thinking strategically, and, as a shareholder, I was encouraged. I did have a twinge of doubt about marketing discretionary products to people who often didn't have access to clean water. I found it troubling. But I, too, was making good money from poverty and jobs were being created by the popularity of tampons.

"So what brings you to Manila?" Charlotte asked. "Barbara tells me you're working on the environmental problems of the Pasig. God knows—it's a mess."

"I'm evaluating a project for the World Bank. The idea is to get ordinary people involved in creating peer pressure to clean up the river. They're trained to use basic water-testing equipment and to report their findings to the Department of Natural Resources, and perhaps the media. This is problematic, because the DNR is considered one of the most corrupt branches of the government."

"Is the river as bad as everyone says?"

"It's worse than you can imagine. You don't need monitoring equipment. Nothing lives in the Pasig. God, it's dangerous just to live in the vicinity. The place is dead and unhealthy—filled with toxic fumes, sewage, and trash."

"So will your work do any good?" she asked.

"I like the concept, but I wonder about the follow-through. There are vested interests here who don't like the idea of citizens reporting what they see. This mess reflects badly on the government. The citizens need funding to continue…"

Charlotte answered the phone.

It was time to meet the big mahoff, the president. We walked down the hall to the large but workaday office of a Filipino gentleman with a kindly demeanor but an incisive focus on profitability. I was impressed with his explanation of the company's plans in Asia, and I was surprised by his knowledge of the polluted Pasig River. His questions about my work were insightful and full of concern about environmental quality. I didn't expect this.

At six o'clock, we left for Charlotte's home in Forbes Park, where the average price of a house is about five million dollars. Rudolpho drove us past the guardhouse, and we entered one of the more elite enclaves in the world. Large mansions with manicured lawns mixed with homes that were merely huge. Charlotte lived in a substantial American-style rancher on an unusually large lot landscaped with tropical plants. This household was tended by a full-time gardener, a part-time cook, and a full-time all-arounder, who did everything else when necessary—cooking, cleaning, child care, running errands, and taking kids to school. Charlotte's home was filled with Asian paintings and the mementos of a life of travel. The tasteful and expensive paintings were professionally arranged, corporate-style. The place was immaculate. It was a little spooky, a little too museumlike for a private home.

Dinner was prepared by Magnolia, a fortyish Filipina, and included a number of local specialties followed by an Australian wine. I enjoyed our wide-ranging discussions and was amazed by Charlotte's knowledge, not only of business but of world politics and literature. I thought she'd have a real chance on *Jeopardy*. She was both opinionated and receptive to new ideas, an unusual combination. I imagined it was difficult to be so well informed while keeping a single-minded focus on selling American tampons to the women of Asia. She asked me questions about how I knew Barbara and how I'd gotten involved with the World Bank. She was trying to figure me out. It was in her DNA, and in mine.

"So where are we going tonight? What's your surprise?" I asked.

"We're going ballroom dancing at the Intercontinental," she said with a cheeky grin.

"What?"

"You'll love it. It's a real hoot. I go frequently on Saturday evenings when I'm in town. It's great exercise and I meet lots of interesting people. It's a good way to keep up with the local gossip."

I was terrified. "But I can't dance. I haven't danced since high school. I've always avoided dancing because I am totally doplick," I said, using a word that people apply to the uncoordinated on my home turf of Pennsylvania. "I'll tell you what, I'll go but just watch," I said.

"No, David, you are going to dance and you're going to like it. There will be absolutely no sitting down—you'll be hustling continuously for three hours!" she said with a stern smile. I wasn't sure if she was putting me on.

"But I'll make a fool of myself, a total ass. I can't do it," I replied.

"Oh, yes, you can. You're not going to make a fool of yourself because I've arranged for you to have a dance instructor. She is a professional dancer, one of the very best. She speaks English as well as we do. You'll be in a ballroom filled with people. The regulars have seen it all. You'll meet some very interesting people, the elite of Philippine society."

My God, she has me, I thought. Sweet Jesus, what am I gonna do now?

Outside, Rudolpho had the limo idling. He could barely contain his laughter. I suspected that he had seen this drama before. I endured the short drive to Makati in a state of deep concern, to put it mildly. We emerged from the limo at 9:10 p.m. I asked Charlotte immediately when the event would end.

"Midnight. On the dot."

Oh, geez, I thought to myself. This is going to be a long evening. I took some solace in knowing that Barbara would not take kindly to my being humiliated, and since Charlotte and Barbara were friends, how bad could it be? Then again, Barbara has a great sense of humor.

Filled with art and marble corridors, the Intercontinental Hotel was a playground for the elite, providing them with extensive business services and security. The hotel's ballroom was crowded—it held a thousand people—and, I would later learn, many dancers brought their own bodyguards. They couldn't be too careful because being kidnapped is an unpleasant and expensive proposition. While it looked pedestrian from the outside, the hotel (the first five-star hotel in Makati) was designed by Philippine national artist Leandro Locsin and exuded power and wealth. It was perfect for the clientele it wished to attract.

We walked through the ornate lobby where Charlotte greeted people, one after the other. A middle-aged man wore an unimpressive jet-black toupee and a *Dragnet*-era suit. An elderly European lady wore a low-cut lace dress from the days of Empire, while another was an elderly Cinderella. It was quite an assembly of egos, of eccentricity. I was starting to think it might be an interesting evening, if only I didn't have to dance.

As we made our way to the crowded elevators and up to the enclosed rooftop ballroom, I stole a quick look at my watch: 9:26. We entered the ballroom to the music of Arturo Sandoval, played by a live orchestra that would've made Guy Lombardo proud. The strobe lights were bright and disorienting, but I felt a little better in the crowd. I could just stand there and not be noticed, at least not much, and there was plenty to look at.

"David, look over there, do you see that woman?' asked

Charlotte.

"You mean the older lady with the man who looks like Ricardo Montalbán?"

"Yes, he's her dance instructor. That's Mrs. Ayala, the family matriarch. She owns this hotel."

Charlotte pointed out a number of wealthy people in the room, most of them women. One had a dance instructor who looked like Liberace's Filipino cousin, another lady was being taught by a dead ringer for Cesar Romero. Many of them wore gowns out of 1940s Hollywood. The men, in business suits and barongs, were huddled together talking strategy, eyeing the young girls, or seeing how much they could drink. Many boasted of business deals, while others openly brainstormed new possibilities. It was pretty campy, pretty weird, but I was starting to get the picture. This was a safe place for the wealthy to mingle and dance with an attractive partner. Powerful men often acquiesced to the wishes of their wives and made the most of the circumstances. Few actually liked dancing and many simply sent their wives with a bodyguard.

Charlotte introduced me to Maria, my knockout of a dance instructor. Like the other instructors, she looked more Spanish than Filipina, and her skin was unusually light for Manila. She was a seductively wholesome woman in her mid-twenties wearing a bright red dress and a knowing smile. Maria was the perfect combination of elegant and foxy with a smart, edgy sense of humor. She was a pistol. Sometimes her expression suggested she knew things that I didn't know, like what the hell was going on.

"You'll be fine," Charlotte said, "I'll check back with you later."

The orchestra struck up a cha-cha. Help, I thought.

"It's so good to meet you, Mr. David. Let's get started."

"Wait a minute. I've got to explain some things first. I'm a total klutz, really. Some people say such things out of modesty, but I assure you I'm serious. I am totally oafish. I'm not coordinated," I said, "except in baseball."

She laughed out loud. "Don't worry," she said, "this isn't difficult. You'll learn quickly."

"I am worried," I said, "and your shoes should be worried."

"Well, you have a good sense of humor. You may need it. Now let's get started," she said snarkily.

"Mr. David, you must actually move your feet, like this," she said, demonstrating. She was a very congenial drill sergeant, and I suspect she had encountered uncoordinated people like me before. She quickly saw that I wasn't kidding, but she did get me moving, even if I ambulated like a zombie. It was ten o'clock and I was beginning to sweat. Poetry in motion did not seem to be happening for me.

I asked her about the dance-instructor business, and I confessed to my growing sense that this event was not a dance but a theater of the absurd. "You think so, Mr. David?"

"Judging from what I have seen so far, absolutely," I said.

"You're right, but you don't know the half of it," she whispered.

She told me she was a teacher in a local high school but danced professionally whenever she could, mostly Saturdays at the Intercontinental when she could manage it. She gave me her card, suggesting that she was interested in corporate work.

During the evening, I received many cards from young women whose day jobs were in insurance, teaching, or nursing. While I couldn't help them, I thought that they had the right idea. If I were a senior executive at the Asian Development Bank, Robinson's or Nestlé Asia, I'd hire these ladies. They were highly intelligent, understood the ironies of life, and laughed at the serious phoniness around them. They knew that the dance was something of a masquerade in which the participants were oblivious to the dire poverty that was a mere couple of blocks from the hotel, where people begged for your half-eaten donut.

Every twenty minutes, Charlotte checked in with me,

probably to make sure that I wasn't having a heart attack, hadn't injured my instructor, and wasn't mad as hell. She'd introduce me to this or that "high one," and then disappear for another twenty minutes. There are a dozen extended families in the Philippines who largely own the country, and that night I met several of them, as well as senators, corporate leaders, and other assorted biggies.

I would have asked for a rest, but thought this would look weak. I scouted for a place to sit down but there were few chairs, and fewer that were not occupied either by old ladies or security. I had no choice but to keep dancing. "How about a drink?" I asked.

"What would you like?"

"A Coke Light or a San Miguel Light," I said. Like magic, a friend of Maria's appeared out of the crowd with my beverage. I had to drink quickly because there was no slacking. Periodically, Maria had a drink, but when she did one of her friends filled in. At first, I thought the girls were laughing at me, and maybe they were. They were also following instructions, making me work hard. But as I got to know them I saw that they were having fun, and I found myself less anxious. They were good at their jobs.

Gradually, I came to realize that I was in charge, that I needed to assert myself. I asked Maria about the menagerie of high ones surrounding me and the ridiculousness of it all: men wearing suits or barongs and sporting Elvis-like pompadours, bejeweled blue-haired matrons in beehives, leering gentlemen, and serious alcoholics. One man reminded me of an elderly John Travolta, with dance moves just as good. It was part circus, part exercise class, part adult day care for the rich and powerful, and part networking venue for the ruling class. It offered potential for dance instructors, too.

Maria soon dropped the "Mr." "David," she said, only half kidding, "you wouldn't believe some of these people. Geniuses, crazy people, eccentrics, they are all here right now. They live in their own world and are oblivious to the community around them. Most of them are not what they seem."

"Just like us," I said.

"Exactly!"

I continued to attempt to dance, while eliciting funny, sometimes disturbing stories about the Filipino elite from Maria and her friends. We laughed together about the absurdity of the dance, yet we all agreed on its value.

At midnight, the lights flickered, soon the orchestra began packing up, and the crowd headed for the elevators. Charlotte appeared and I asked if I should give Maria a tip. She indicated that tips were unnecessary. "Absolutely not more than five hundred pesos."

"How about the assistant instructors?'

Charlotte was adamant. "No. Well, maybe a hundred pesos each. That's it."

I gave a thousand pesos to Maria and a couple hundred to the other three. They seemed surprised but appreciative, and they encouraged me to return for more laughs.

"I'm just visiting," I said, "I'm no dancer."

"Maybe not, David, but you could be. You showed great improvement," one said with a sly smile. "This was fun, wasn't it? You should come back."

"Maybe," I said, "when I'm back in Manila."

"Admit it, David. You had a good time. Admit it!" Charlotte said later.

"Well, I lost ten pounds," I said.

"No, admit that you had a good time."

"I did," I said.

"I knew you would," she said, breaking into laughter.

Fungus In Paradise

"Oh, God! Get off of the floor. That looks gross! Why are you barefoot? Take that wheelchair…What is it? What happened?" Thus asked the young nurse at the Lancaster General Hospital around midnight on a sticky August evening in my home region of southeastern Pennsylvania. She was disconcerted—not a good sign.

"I was hoping you'd be able to tell *me*," I said bluntly. "I'm really messed up. I just got off the plane from Manila. I can't get my shoes back on—not even close. God, it hurts to walk."

My feet and lower legs were covered with a psychedelic display of what looked like starfish, snakes, and baseballs. Some were dark, some transparent, and others translucent, all raised and covering fiery red skin. It was quite a sight. To make matters worse, my feet itched and I had scratched them. The sores exuded a river of fluids, led by a torrent of pus. They looked like something from *Night of the Living Dead*.

"The doctor will see you right away," the nurse said, wheeling me into a dispiriting and cluttered ER.

A young, pudgy doctor in a white coat appeared within a couple of minutes, and he did not inspire my confidence. He looked like a kid. How much would he know about oddball tropical diseases?

"I've had this for a couple of weeks and it keeps getting

worse," I said. "I just got back from Manila. I was treated there, but they were puzzled—the doctor figured that my disease was another odd infection that unprepared tourists acquire. He gave me a few days' worth of antibiotics and wished me well. Geez, I feel like I have a total body infection. My feet were only slightly enlarged when I got on the plane, now look at them! Not only that, my ear's infected and I can't hear well."

The doctor examined my feet and ears. "I don't know what it started as, but it's turned into cellulitis. We can admit you and put you on IV antibiotics, or you can take your chances at home on heavy-duty medication. Either way, you'll need large doses for several weeks. You're lucky that you came here quickly, otherwise you'd have gone into septicemia."

He gave me a couple shots then asked, "Where did you go in the Philippines? I haven't seen anything like this before. It's unusual, probably a tropical infection on top of some underlying condition caused by who knows what…We don't need to know what kind—the treatment is the same."

I told him how the pus had oozed copiously through my leather shoes, weakening me. I'd always liked those shoes, but ended up throwing them away in a dumpster at Harrison Plaza mall in Ermita, walking instead in sandals along the polluted streets of Manila. Sometimes all options are bad. Sometimes there is a price to be paid for entering paradise. I told him about the punctured eardrum and subsequent infection, the bats and their guano, the polluted ocean, the strange insects and all the rest. I told him about our visit to the "Last Frontier," the remote island of Palawan. This was 1998 and calling it that was not a stretch. Let's just say that it exceeded my expectations.

"When you come in August, you may want to take a side trip to Palawan," my son Andrew had suggested. As a Peace Corps volunteer near Manila, he knew some stuff about the country, especially unusual regions frequented by fellow volunteers. "It's a striking place, one of the most biologically diverse locations in the world. It's relatively undeveloped, but you can fly there from Manila. It has some great beaches and an interesting mix of people. And, it is in the very early stages of development. You should go while you can."

"Is it safe?" Marilyn asked.

"Oh, sure. The Peace Corps has several volunteers there, mainly at the underground river."

"Underground river?"

"Yes. It's supposedly one of the wonders of the world. You'd take a small boat through the cave section of the Cabayugan River for about five kilometers. There's a huge chamber with thousands of bats and spectacular stalactites and stalagmites. It's amazing. And not many people go there."

We were tempted. Like Costa Rica when we went there in 1978, the island of Utila in Honduras in 1984, and Czechoslovakia in 1985, Palawan was ripe for exploitation. It had the trappings to attract upscale resorts and the modernization to keep folks coming back. Sunshine, warmth, beaches, natural beauty, unusual geography, and a feeling of being in an exotic place are a seductive combination. We'd need to go there quickly if we wanted to see the old Palawan.

We began to research this oasis at the end of the world, 5500 square miles of largely uncrowded beaches and forests on a long, slender island inhabited by 600,000 people, including several aboriginal tribes. Ecologically, Palawan was much like Borneo, featuring over two hundred species of birds, a host of mammals, and an overwhelming agglomeration of vegetation. It was also the habitat of a huge array of insects, endemic malaria, and other diseases. We decided to take some antimalarial drugs, just in case.

After a few days with Andrew, we boarded our Philippine Air flight to Puerto Princesa, the capital of Palawan. We were accustomed to the feel and the smells of small Filipino airports, overcrowded and antiquated, with the scents of tropical fruit, tobacco smoke, and fried chicken coalescing with human sweat and generalized pollution. The ancient Puerto Princesa facility didn't dampen our eagerness.

After a short van ride down dusty, pocked dirt roads surrounded by lush plant growth, we arrived at our destination, the Palawan Inn. This was an unexpectedly modern hotel without much hot water but with a dense tropical garden fronting the lobby atrium. We ordered drinks, sat down on the bamboo chairs, and began to observe the local fauna. There weren't many guests, but we did see a few Australians as well as an older American man and a couple of Filipino families on holiday. As we considered the beauty of the garden, I swatted an insect from my face and soon noticed that the left side of my forehead had begun to swell. In less than a minute an egg-sized lump appeared.

"My God," I said, "what if this thing keeps growing?"

"You can actually see it getting bigger," Marilyn said. "You need to go somewhere."

"And where would that be?"

Just as quickly as it had appeared, the bulge vanished. I had taken a sinus pill an hour before—maybe that helped, maybe it saved me from serious illness…We learned one thing from the experience: watch out for the bugs of Palawan. When you venture into the wild, go prepared.

We began to explore the city. It was not what we expected. It was crowded, poor, dusty, and scorching, and it felt like it harbored disease, but it had its compensations. It was sensual, exuding a delightful bouquet of dust, exhaust fumes, fried chicken, and the sea, and felt almost unreal. The town itself offered little more than the basics of life, save for an excellent collection of eclectic restaurants, strong on fish and fruit dishes. The local people moved slowly in the midday tropical sun, but they smiled at you in the din of *jeepney* horns (jeepneys are a combination of a jeep and a bus) and revving tricycle motors.

The population was as diverse as the flora, with over eighty distinct cultural groups, including people from Borneo, Malaysia, China, and the Middle East. There were Muslims, Christians, and Bataks, a mountain-dwelling people originally from Sumatra. We were impressed by the tolerance and sense of community that seemed to prevail on the island, where only a third of the population spoke the national language, Tagalog. It was strictly live-and-let-live, and folks cooperated, whether it was fixing a jeepney or preparing a meal in a restaurant. It all seemed to work, and everyone had a role to play in this remote world. Everyone was doing *something*.

We went to a combination of café and used bookstore and struck up a conversation with the proprietor, an Englishman who was quite literate, if unkempt. Yes, he said, it sometimes gets very hot on Palawan, and yes, the malaria is uncontrolled. He didn't take prophylactic measures to thwart the disease, however, indicating he'd rather take his chances. There wasn't much in the way of medical care on the island anyway. He enjoyed his existence in the sun without sunscreen, but with a double-malt chaser. He seemed happy, if bored, as did the Peace Corps volunteers who hit the bookstore on weekends away from the underground river; it was a prime watering hole for expats in Puerto Princesa.

"You guys work at the underground river?" I asked two of the patrons.

"Yeah, it's pretty dead," said one, a scruffy guy from Ohio. "But it's a beautiful place. Of course, you could go nuts. There aren't many visitors and just a couple of park security guards. We've been making signs to direct the few tourists, printing brochures, that kind of thing. Otherwise we just hang out, drink a little.

We come here on weekends. There are several volunteers on the other side of the city—it's a good central meeting place. And Puerto Princesa can get pretty interesting late at night."

He had traveled the island. "Palawan isn't perfect. There's illegal deforestation. Heck, some people cut down the mangroves for firewood. The locals love meat and hunt almost everything, including endangered species. We're supposed to be educators, but I don't know if anyone pays any attention to us. We do hold classes for kids and adults. We've developed educational games and pamphlets that we spread around the island."

"It sounds like you're making progress," Marilyn observed.

"Yeah, I do think that there's been some improvement in people's awareness of the environment. And there's no doubt that local officials see the potential for lots of cash coming from ecotourism," he said.

"What else can they do?" Marilyn asked.

"You can't blame them for thinking along those lines. There really isn't any alternative," I said.

"You're probably right," he replied. "Developers are already scouting the area. We'll have lots of resorts—after I'm gone."

"Yep," said another volunteer, "go down to the main beach and you'll see what we mean. It's a beautiful place, but it's rough. They need money—they need tourists' dollars."

We headed for Parola Beach, the nearest one to town. Crowded, with intermittent trash scattered about, it nonetheless offered spectacular scenery, soothing blue water, and warm sunshine. It lacked facilities and infrastructure: it was rough, but one could easily envision its future as a world-class resort. Encouraging signs dotted the area with plastic placards reminding folks to pick up trash and to keep the island a paradise. You could see the beginning of the "greening" of the island, the start of "ecological development," and perhaps we were among the first ecotourists. Like Costa Rica in the late 1970s, the potential for leveraging a relatively unspoiled environment into jobs and infrastructure was an obvious way out of poverty for the many and the means of enrichment for a few.

The next morning we headed to the market, where we found some colorful, happy local art mixed in with the fish, coconuts, rice, and fruit. Marilyn bought a Palawan landscape painted on a recycled piece of plywood with metal backing hung by a piece of string, probably made from leftover construction material. We saw bicycle shops serving the large tricycle trade, small family-run *sari-sari* stores selling groceries out of their homes, and the usual workaday flotsam of poor cities in poor countries, as well as a number of government buildings, since this was the provincial capital.

In some ways, it was as if a tiny slice of Metro Manila had been dropped into the center of a pristine island paradise, displacing the aboriginal inhabitants and infecting the place with Filipino politics: not quite colonial, not quite kosher. The island, we found, was largely untouched, but rough-edged Puerto Princesa had its share of big-city problems.

Walking around the town in sneakers and white socks, my feet began to itch. Badly. Periodically, I had to remove my Vans to scratch my feet. I must have an infection, I thought, as the small blisters multiplied. I suspected athlete's foot, perhaps picked up from the hotel shower.

The next day we headed for the underground river, officially the Puerto Princesa Subterranean River National Park. It was a thirty-mile ride in a small jeepney with a local driver and another couple, but it took almost four hours on a meandering unpaved road. The ride zigzagged around fallen trees, large rocks, and the occasional dead animal. The journey passed through areas of dense jungle rife with a medley of snakes, parrots, monkeys, and lizards. The biomass was overpowering—there was life everywhere—and combined with the periodic jolts from the jeepney, disorienting. We were in another world.

We passed aboriginal tribes with women hanging their bright clothes out to dry and men chopping wood in a haze of grayish smoke from a stone stove. Once Palawan was discovered, we wondered how these people would fare when they came face-to-face with modernity. Perhaps they'd learn to clean hotel rooms at a new Marriott or they would give anthropological tours. I couldn't help thinking of the former headhunter I'd met near Baguio, in northern Luzon, who wore a Detroit Pistons T-shirt and earned his living by charging for pictures with tourists.

Entering the park we followed handmade signs to the river's edge, waded through the water, and boarded a small wooden boat with a guide. Six of us, all foreigners, flashlights in hand, paddled our way through the tunnel-like entrance, enveloped in a sulfuric-smelling cocoon of bat guano fumes. Our guide steered the boat along the narrow passage under the limestone outcropping. We slowly traversed a narrow river, entering the cavern, surrounded by thousands of wheeling, swarming bats swooshing past our heads. The ancient outcroppings looked surreal, yellow, brown, and red: they formed shapes resembling animals, buildings, and even the Virgin Mary. As we drifted in the water, the silence was broken only by the droppings of the swifts and the bats which could be heard faintly, as if we were in the midst of a gentle rain. Occasionally a bat flew close to us, a frightening experience given the surroundings. Otherwise, it was like staring into an abyss, spooky, especially in the overcrowded wooden boat. We were exhausted by the heat, the humidity, and oxygen deprivation in the cave; we were all as heavily speckled with guano as were the cavern walls. But it was a twelve-hour adventure worth taking: it was why we'd come.

Back at the hotel, when I removed my saturated socks and Vans, my by-now soggy feet were covered in sores that itched like hell.

"Keep your feet dry and take your antihistamines," Marilyn warned. "You don't want an infection. You should've worn sandals so your feet could breathe…And don't scratch." She was concerned and pretty good with her ex post facto advice. We were leaving for Manila the next day, so I could get medical care there if I needed to.

When Andrew met us at the Manila airport, I told him about my feet.

"I spoke with Joe, he can take us swimming in Nagsuba in Batangas Province. The salt water should help your feet. It's a nice place, close to Manila. We can spend a couple days there. How's that sound?"

We thought that it sounded pretty good, and at less than two hours away, manageable.

The next afternoon we found ourselves on the beach, waiting for Andrew's boss Joe to fetch a small boat. We spent two days in Nagsuba, and I was careful to keep my feet in the water. I even tried snorkeling. We hung out on the boat, and I enjoyed my Coke Light and Savinelli tobacco pipe, feeling blessed by the sun. The water was clear and the view of the neighboring hills soothing. At least my feet had stopped itching.

Later that night my eardrum perforated, possibly from the snorkeling, or perhaps from the flight from Palawan. Déjà vu. Max Ronis, a sinus specialist at Temple University, once told me, "Dave, you have bum eustachian tubes. You can't do anything about it. Just keep your head above water." Sometimes I'm not so good at following instructions.

To make things worse, my feet were badly infected, and I wondered about the cleanliness of the ocean water around Nagsuba, relatively close to the polluted Manila Bay. When we returned to Manila, we headed for Doctors Hospital. With pus oozing from my leather hiking shoes, I felt like I had the plague. As to the perforated eardrum, I was told there was nothing that could be done about that, because it had not, as yet, become infected, and I was given standard, minimal therapy.

"We don't treat this condition with antibiotics prophylactically, only if there's an infection," the Filipino doctor said.

"But aren't the odds of infection pretty high, especially in Manila?"

"If you get an infection in your ear, come back and we can treat it. Hopefully it will heal by itself. As to your feet, you have an infection and possibly a fungal condition. I'll give you a few days' worth of antibiotics for your feet and some pills for pain. I'll give you some ointment as well. When do you leave?"

"I have two more days in Manila."

After bandaging my feet, he suggested that I seek medical attention as soon as I returned home. My feet worsened and two days later I hobbled onto the airplane with a budding ear infection. My visit to the emergency room at Doctors had been useless, but the price was right: less than six dollars. Maybe you get what you pay for.

My visit to the ER in Lancaster took care of the cellulitis. While the ear infection cleared quickly, it took almost a year for the infection in my sinuses to fully subside. The foot infection came and went, never clearing up completely. I tried everything I could think of. I made an appointment with a podiatrist who sagely observed, "That's nasty stuff, you really should see someone." Increasingly powerful antibiotics prescribed by an ENT physician seemed finally to put the infection to rest. It took a full year.

Still, sixteen years later, when it is hot and my feet sweat, a cluster of bubbles appears on them. The underlying disease, this Filipino rot, ebbs and flows. I've learned that dryness and sunshine keep the beast at bay, so I try to act accordingly. I try to follow instructions.

A couple of years ago I asked Alain Rook, a dermatologist at the University of Pennsylvania, to have a look at my foot fungus and tell me what he thought.

"Can't say, unless it is active. It sounds like something other than a fungus, but it could be. I'd have to see it when it's active," he said.

I visited him again six months later with active bubbles.

"Yes, you need to treat this, contain it," he said. "I think that it's eczema, not a fungus."

Several months later I was being treated by dermatologist Bruce Brod in Lancaster, Pennsylvania.

"How about having a look at my foot fungus?" I asked. "It isn't active, but it recently was. You can see the remnants," I said, pointing to the residue.

"I don't think it's a foot fungus, it's something else," he said.

"I think it's a fungus," I replied. "It acts like a fungus."

"I'm almost sure that it is not a fungus, but we can find out for sure. I'll take a sample and send it to the lab. How would that be?"

"Good. Definitive. I'd like that," I said.

A week later I received a call from Dr. Brod.

"I have your lab results. I can tell you, for sure, it's not a fungus. It's probably eczema."

As it turned out, this took nearly a year and a slew of dermatologists, otolaryngologists, podiatrists and internal medicine specialists to control, to contain. The sinuses proved the last bastion of the disease, whatever it was. Surrounded by bone, sinus infections are sometimes tough to treat, but the sinus doctor persevered and ultimately prevailed.

After more than a decade the disease lingers. I've learned to manage the inevitable flare-ups, and it's become simply another of life's tolerable aggravations. My Filipino rot is an enduring souvenir of a vanished time and place. It's a constant reminder of my stay in paradise so many years ago. When you travel widely you acquire many such keepsakes.

Fungus in Paradise

Adriane In Ternate

"I'd like your cheapest brand of cigarettes, light, filtered, hard pack," Adriane said to the clerk. Whispering under her breath, she told us, "I just hate soft packs, they're awful. I like my cigarettes in one piece, and I've gotta have a smoke."

"All our cigarettes in soft packs are seventy pesos, but we only have Marlboro and Camel in the hard packs, and they are seventy-four."

"I'll have two packs of the Camels."

She'd greeted us enthusiastically on her arrival, but seeing a smoke shop out of the corner of her eye…well, first things first. This was her initial trip to the Philippines, although Marilyn and I had been to the country several times. Adriane was anxious to visit her brother, who was here as a Peace Corps volunteer, and to have a family reunion. As their parents, we were looking forward to time with our children, who were growing in different ways: Andrew the responsible environmentalist, Adriane the artist specializing in metalwork.

Adriane had just disembarked from a Philippine Air flight from L.A., and she was a little unhinged. This was, no doubt, due to a ten-hour regimen of rum and Cokes with San Miguel chasers, followed by the inevitable smoke, this being 1997 when such things were possible. She was exhausted and wired, and her tired blue eyes darted around the frenzied Manila airport.

The stench of polluted air and sweat mixed with the throngs of people searching for rides, purchasing bus tickets, or looking to change money.

"So how was your flight?" I asked.

"Geez, Louise. So, I was sitting in the near-empty smoking section with these two guys, both very pervy. One must have been at least seventy, an American guy. He was going to visit his girlfriend, who he claimed was eighteen. He said that he provided aircon and some cash for her family, and then he tells me he's on the lookout for more girls. Skinny, balding, he looked like the preacher man from *Poltergeist*. The other guy, much younger, was Australian, wearing a cowboy outfit. Said straight out he was a sex tourist. Can you believe this stuff?"

"Actually, yes. If you look around town you'll see lots of old American men with young Filipinas. They can live here cheaply, don't have to work, and can attract young girls. You may not like it, but it's the reality here. Just pay attention and be careful," I cautioned her.

"When are we going to Ternate? And how the hell are we going to get there?"

Marilyn said that we'd stay the night at the Admiral Hotel down by Manila Bay, then visit Andrew on the following day. We hailed a cab, and in a couple of hours we were ensconced at the hotel after a mediocre dinner at the greasy spoon next door.

Adriane hadn't finished her fruit plate, so after completing our meal we'd left her there discussing the day's events with an American couple who were staying at the hotel. The next morning she told us that she'd enjoyed some after-hours pot, compliments of the management. She'd also spent a couple of hours playing pool with the Americans and a local man who'd said he was a witch, that he could make things levitate, although he never did.

The next morning we boarded a bus for the four-hour, thirty-six-mile trip to the small fishing village of Ternate in neighboring Cavite Province, where Andrew worked. The bus filled immediately with passengers lugging mounds of packages, mostly cardboard boxes overflowing with the stuff of life. It was laborious to breathe on the bus, despite the aircon, and many folks stood munching squid balls or drinking bottled water. Some spoke English, the majority conversed in Tagalog. Most were good natured, lively, and seemingly immune to the tropical heat and exhaust fumes. Dressed in T-shirts and jeans, they were sweaty and tired, but joyful.

Every half hour or so, as the bus stopped to pick up and discharge passengers, vendors descended upon us. You could buy holy cards with paeans to the Blessed Virgin, donuts covered with coconut, *balut* (duck embryos, boiled alive and eaten in the shell), ice cream, T-shirts, toys, or Coca-Cola. We were almost overpowered by the bright colors, the incessant milling crowds of people, by full-throttled life. As the bus moved on, Adriane remarked that the hordes looked like "bugs on the windshield," a sea of insignificant humanity swarming like insects, working, traveling, eating, socializing. She was mesmerized and disoriented, but, at the same time, engrossed in the drama. She was also hungry and wondered about the fare on offer. "What is this stuff? Is it safe?" she asked, pointing to the buko.

"This is amazing," Adriane said, swaying with the bus and peeling a mango given to her by a fellow passenger, "but there are so many people on this bus. God, it's hot."

We stepped off the bus just past the bridge outside of Ternate and were greeted by Andrew: "Welcome to Ternate! How was the bus ride?"

"Andy! God, I never thought that I'd get off that bus. What an experience! You look good, but you've lost weight."

We began our short walk to his *buhay*—Momma Lolain's house. Adriane was greeted by whistles and waves from the young people, that is, most of the town. They screamed at her, although she couldn't understand most of what was being said.

"*Tagpia ni?*" one asked, meaning "How much?" Another shouted "*Gusoka makigsayau konoca,*" "Do you want to dance?"

"Do you know these people, Andy? Who are they?" she asked.

"Oh, just people from the neighborhood."

Clearly, few of them had ever seen an American woman who was so attractive, so uncommon. Few foreigners visit Ternate, and those who pass through are usually looking for directions to the nearby Puerto Azul resort. Andrew simply laughed. He knew that a tattooed American woman with a cigarette would be the highlight of the week for these folks.

"They don't know what to make of you, Adriane," he said, translating their words. "They aren't sure if you are a movie star like Claire Danes or some kind of bad girl."

"You need to put that thing out when we get to Lolain's; she doesn't like smoking," Andrew added, and Adriane for once obeyed. She twisted the butt, sifting the remaining tobacco to the ground, then placed the filter in her pocket. Adriane didn't like litter.

The villagers couldn't get enough of gawking at Adriane. Her appearance and demeanor, like a naughty celebrity's, unnerved them. She had the whitest skin this side of Iceland, dyed blue-black hair, robin's-egg-blue eyes, and several tattoos, including *The Scream*, conspicuous on her back. She was dressed in a long, black tank top, worn jeans, and sandals, which she imagined would help her blend in. She wasn't blending in. "I feel like a rock star, like the Beatles," she said, "but it is a little scary."

Andrew, in near hysterics, explained that to the townsfolk, young ladies who smoked, had tattoos, and dyed their hair were usually prostitutes, although they might be movie stars. She didn't appreciate his interpretation, but what the hell, she was who she was.

Momma Lolain was an anomaly in Ternate herself, a sixty-something widow who dressed formally while everyone else wore jeans, T-shirts, and flip-flops. Her hair was as grey as her skin was smooth—clearly she had kept out of the sun. Unlike her mostly Roman Catholic neighbors, she attended the Inglesia ni Cristo Church, a back-to-the-Bible kind of faith. We were happy that our son, Andrew, had rented a room from her, although her neat and sturdy home was without a telephone and hosted prodigious numbers of diminutive ants. Adriane didn't like insects and brushed them off when they came near her. Momma Lolain ignored this but was, I think, a little offended. Ants are a fact of life and you simply live with them, a fact that Andrew was quick to point out to her.

"Sorry, Andy, I didn't know. How do you live here? I couldn't do it—I like my comfort too much. I do like the geckos, though."

"It's basic, but comfortable. Not bad for the Peace Corps."

"So, what's there to do in this town?" Adriane asked Andrew and Lolain, while sipping an after-dinner iced tea on the veranda.

"You've gotta get a haircut from Cezar. He'll do your nails, too, and tell your fortune." Adriane didn't quite trust her brother's advice, but she was intrigued. She'd always been interested in the supernatural, and she believed in reincarnation.

Momma Lolain said primly: "He is an excellent artist, but his talk of a 'third eye' is blasphemous. You could walk down to the water and watch the fishermen or go over to the park to see the new pavilion," she offered, providing safer alternatives.

"Third eye?" Adriane asked, beguiled.

"Yes, he claims to have a third eye in the middle of his forehead. It's funny, no one else can see it."

"Well, I could use a trim. When does he open for business?"

"In the morning around ten."

We were awakened early, by the sounds of cocks crowing, tricycles revving, and chunky middle-aged female fruit and fish vendors setting up shop across the street under the weathered corrugated metal roof of the outdoor market. Momma Lolain prepared a breakfast of rice, mung beans, fish, and mango, and after our morning meal, we decided to have a look around town, waving to the perspiring women, who stared at us from the shade, but nonetheless waved back. The circus had come to town.

Dusty, fishy, and humid, the town swarmed with happy and inquisitive small children. If we lifted a camera, they lined up perfectly to participate in the picture-taking session. The homes were well kept, a kind of sufferable poverty. Some buildings were constructed of concrete but many were cobbled together from wood and other cheaply available flotsam. Most looked vulnerable to the inevitable typhoon. We saw signs advertising chicken feed, movies, a Catholic church event, and the Miss Gay Ternate pageant.

As we walked, a man with a moustache fluttered by quickly in front of us, dressed in a flowing white wedding gown. He passed before I could comprehend what I had just seen. Andrew knew the man and said his name was Reagan.

"This is so cool," Adriane said. "People here are pretty open, which I would never have thought, and the place is kind of funky."

We walked to the outskirts of town and then turned back. It was nine thirty and Cezar would soon be open. His shop was just around the corner from Lolain's, but before reaching Cezar's we visited the open-air market, where we were greeted with cries of "Look here" and "Special for you." We visited each stall, purchasing fruit at what Andrew claimed were inflated prices, while the vendors glanced surreptitiously at Adriane. She was a sight, but also a good customer, picking up a bag of mangos, some papayas, sunscreen, a hard pack of cheap Filipino cigarettes, and a kilo of fish that she would later offer to a few of the town's many tailless cats.

We found Cezar's salon, which was housed in a small concrete building across from the market. Behind the peeling door, we entered a fashionable parlor with a barber chair, several stations for hair drying, and a table and chair used for pedicures and manicures. We were greeted by the effusive, hyperactive Cezar, who welcomed us as his first customers of the day.

Cezar had long, stylishly coiffed hair, a large gap between his front teeth, and a flamboyant friendliness that drew us to him. His most distinguishing characteristic was not his "third eye," invisible to us just as Momma Lolain had predicted, but his pointy, shaped, and lacquered toenails.

"We'd all like to get our hair cut," Marilyn said to him.

"Yes," he said, turning to me, "you are the one most in need. I'll start with you."

"Cezar," I said, "I'll pass on the pedicure. But I'll have a haircut and maybe some predictions from your 'third eye.'"

"So, you know about my third eye. Some don't believe it, but I can tell you something about your future. I can see it, I can see your soul with this eye," he said, pointing to the center of his forehead.

As Cezar cut my hair, he observed that it grew "improperly," that I'd never have nice hair. He'd do what he could. As for my fortune, I'd have a life filled with successes and adversities. I wasn't impressed with his hair cutting or his fortune telling, but I liked *him*, a real character.

Cezar cautioned Adriane about using too much "wrong color" hair dye and predicted an interesting and productive, if chaotic, life for her.

"How did you know that my life will be chaotic? It always has been, you know..."

"You, like me, are an artist. There is nothing more to say," he observed with a sly smile.

"Well, what's wrong with the color, Cezar?" Adriane asked.

"It's much too harsh for your light skin. And it hides your eyes, rather than emphasizing them. A light brown or blonde would be better."

Dirty blonde was Adriane's natural hair color, but she was easily bored and liked to experiment: natural just didn't work for her.

Andrew had his standard haircut. He was clearly a regular. Marilyn had a trim and a pedicure, unusual for her, and enjoyed the proceedings, if not necessarily the result. Cezar said that she had "lousy hair" too, but that he'd do his best to give her a pixie. By the time we'd finished, several women were waiting for pedicures. They laughed and joked with us—they were regulars, too.

It was late morning when we left the salon, and we were confronted by the intense tropical heat and an army of jeepneys with signs touting Vanilla Ice, the Chicago Cubs, and, of course, Jesus. We headed back to the market for cold drinks. Despite the heat, the vendors of fried pork, fish sandwiches, mangos, donuts, and buckets of chicken seemed to be doing well, and they offered refuge from the sun.

Adriane, seeing a small boy struggling to obtain water from the town pump, rushed out to help him. She put her full weight, perhaps 110 pounds, into the effort, and although she was successful, she gashed her right foot grappling with the pump. Fortunately, there was a Band-Aid seller right at the market. While the bandages didn't entirely do the job, they helped.

We spent most of our time in Ternate exploring the village and its immediate environs, sights like a rope bridge that had appeared in films; the decaying Puerto Azul resort, once a mecca for wealthy Japanese golfers; and the usual small daily events that were part of the town culture. In only a few days, Adriane became part of the town and a celebrity of sorts. Now kids shouted "Adriane! Adriane!" And she would stop to chat with them, taking pictures and laughing. She was a star.

One afternoon, Adriane asked Andrew, "What else is there to do around here? God, I'd love a cold beer."

So Andrew took Adriane to Chick-to-Chick, a lonely,

windowless building on the outskirts of town, away from the houses. When they entered, they were the only customers. Adriane confided to me later that the drab walls were decorated with Filipino girly posters. Numerous, mostly rough-looking middle-aged women played cards in the dim light under dusty ceiling fans. They liked working at Chick-to-Chick, although they didn't seem to have anything to do.

They looked up to acknowledge the visitors as Adriane and Andrew sat down on old metal chairs covered with red vinyl at ancient wooden tables. Under the glass tops could be seen the limited menu on offer: beer, mixed drinks, chicken and pork dishes. Filipinoized country music droned in the background and later a Perry Como wannabe provided a serenade. Occasionally, one of the women would amble over to the refrigerator to retrieve a drink. Business was slow.

"What would you like?"

"I'll have a San Miguel," Adriane said.

"A San Mig Light," her brother said.

"Andy, where the hell are we?"

"Where do you think?"

"Feels like some kind of hooker hell. Is this the best we can do? Is it safe? At least the beer is cold..."

Andrew explained that the place had many faces. For some, it was simply a place to escape the heat and have a cold beer. For others…And, yes, it was safe during the day. Peace Corps volunteers frequented the place from the area around Ternate— all eight of them, most living in nearby Maragondon. "Hey," he said, "the beer is good, and we're close to town. This is as good as it gets in Ternate." Adriane later said that that wasn't very good, but nonetheless, she enjoyed talking with the rough but interesting women.

Over the course of the week, we managed to meet most of the Peace Corps volunteers: a doctor's son from New York, a graduate of Columbia; a middle-aged woman from the Midwest who had majored in art; an older woman, a serial volunteer who had served in many countries and who was never going back to the United States. They gave us a number of perspectives on the place. All agreed that the people were poor, the environmental situation precarious, health care minimal, and that for most, there was little hope of improving their lot…Yet, all told us that the people seemed happy, that they embraced life.

Adriane liked the volunteers, particularly the artist who was working with an art cooperative over in Maragondon, advising local artisans about marketing their work in Manila. She had difficulty understanding how, in the midst of poverty, the locals could be less anxious about life than the volunteers or she herself. They seemed less pressured, despite their economic circumstances, more accepting of the monotony of daily life. But she still didn't think that she could actually live in Ternate.

Before we left town, I asked Adriane about her impressions.

"Well, I hate the bugs, the heat, and humidity, and that the locals add sugar to almost everything, even bread. Can you believe it? I don't like the poverty, trash thrown everywhere, or the cats without tails—that's really weird."

"There must be some things you like, after all you'll have to admit that you've had some fun."

"Oh, sure. They are really tolerant here, once they get to know you. I like the geckos, the fresh fruit, and the friendly people. They seem real."

She was especially impressed by the ultraneat appearance of the schoolchildren, so well groomed in their crisp white shirts and ironed pants and skirts, despite being almost peso-less.

As we walked to the bus stop, folks greeted her and wished her a good trip. "When are you coming back, Adriane?" some asked.

"Maybe next year."

"Would you really like to come back?" Andrew asked.

"Absolutely. It would be better if we stayed at the resort,

though."

Adriane's foot was getting worse every day, and we were becoming concerned. Back in Manila, she had it examined at Manila Doctors Hospital. MDH looked and felt like the 1950s despite the fact that it was 1997. Though crowded and antiquated, it functioned more or less efficiently. The doctor indicated that Adriane's foot was badly infected and issued a prescription for antibiotics: the total cost of her treatment was about five dollars. Leaving the hospital, we headed for the upscale SM Megamall in Ortigas for a cold drink at Starbucks, and, as Adriane put it, "a little taste of America."

The following day, when we entered the Manila airport to see Adriane off, we noticed that she seemed copacetic and looked significantly different than when she had arrived. With shorter hair, flip-flops, and a sunburn, she was now oblivious to the circus around us: "Do you think I'll be able to get buko juice in Carbondale?"

"I'll bet you'll see coconut water at Kroger," Marilyn offered, "but watch out for the mangos. They're from Central America and don't taste as good."

Before boarding her flight, Adriane stopped at the smoke shop for a hard pack of Camels. This time she had a relaxed conversation with the woman behind the counter.

"Why is it that you are so insistent on the hard pack? You'd get better prices and have a greater selection if you were more flexible."

"It's more economical to have cigarettes that I can shove in my pocket without breaking," Adriane said with a laugh.

We walked our daughter to the departure gate, and we all noticed several older American men, traveling alone or with young Filipina companions.

"They creep me out…Geez, I hope I don't have to sit next to one of those guys—it's a ten-hour flight. It's funny that we didn't see anyone like that in Ternate. I wonder why?"

"Maybe it is too isolated, too poor to attract foreigners," I explained. "Maybe they'd be uncomfortable around so many relatives and neighbors, so many inquisitive eyes."

Adriane in Ternate

A Good Meal

The intersection of Padre Faure and Mabini in Ermita is pleasant enough during the day, with fruit vendors, local hangers-on, myriad homeless children begging for a few coins, and the bright colors and smells of a tropical megalopolis. Businessmen, University of the Philippines students, and tourists mix easily with a sea of poor people and permanent traffic gridlock. Automobile fumes combine with fried chicken, donuts, tropical fruit, sweat, and sewage to create a sensory paradise. When I'm there I know I'm alive.

In the evening everything changes, with trolls emerging from backstreets into the sultry night air to mingle with panhandlers, petty criminals, and prostitutes. The 7-Eleven on the corner is the only place to buy a Coke Light, unless you want to enter the Cowboy Bar, a couple of blocks away, where patrons check their guns at the door. The Cowboy is a busy place, and its bright exterior lighting invites folks to congregate, drink, and laugh the night away. It offers an eclectic array of Filipino bands playing US-style country music; late at night there are drag-queen bands and things get a little crazy.

Across the street at the bank, some local denizens sleep in cardboard boxes or stretch out on the steps. There is construction next to the bank, and some folks sack out in the giant concrete building cylinders or in shopping carts. It's the dry season and everything is cool. In the morning the workaday world will return.

I approach the worn-out 7-Eleven cautiously, in the throes of a sea of desperate and despairing people. I see a shriveled and lethargic woman dressed in rags sitting on the sidewalk in front of the store, holding an emaciated cat. She is eating a Krispy Kreme donut and nods to me as I stop to pet the friendly but weak creature. The cat offers his best, if pathetic, greeting, and I walk warily into the cramped store. I weave tentatively through the loiterers, down the aisle to the refrigerated section in the back, retrieving a Coke Light. I look around, spy a can of tuna fish with a pop-top, and take my purchases to the cash register in front. A somnambulant woman in a San Francisco 49ers T-shirt rings me up without looking at me, and I leave the store. Once outside, I hand the can of tuna to the woman. "It's for your cat," I say, pointing at the animal.

The woman looks up with one opened eye: "The cat?"

"Yes, he needs to eat."

She accepts the can, staring vacantly at me.

The vagrants sitting menacingly next to her on the sidewalk burst into laughter: "Why do you give food to a cat?" one asks.

"It looks like it could use a good meal," I reply, hustling toward my hotel.

"How about a beer for me, Joe?" one shouts.

"Old Manila" is changing, and the downtrodden business district is now pocked with upscale boutiques, luxury hotels, construction, and new money. Soon many of the local people will have to move, but where will they go? Here, they know how to survive and have built their own community. What will happen to them when they move on?

Rockwell

"I selected a condo on a low floor, so I can't see the poor people on the other side of the wall," said Augusta, a congenial sixty-something Malaysian who lives on the third floor here at the Rockwell. Wearing a red micro bikini top, a green wraparound sarong, and a laconic smile, she was en route to the Power Plant Mall, an upscale shopping experience for the "high ones," complete with a guarded private entrance for Rockwell residents. Augusta knew that poor people exist, and she wished them well—she just didn't want to look at them: except, of course, the obsequious employees of the Rockwell, who served her every need for a buck and a half an hour. The Wall at the Rockwell was hidden by tropical trees and plants that were tastefully maintained. I'd been at the Rockwell for more than a week before I realized that there was a wall.

At the Rockwell, in Makati, Metro Manila, life is good for those who can afford it. Condos start at nearly one million dollars and rentals at about five thousand dollars a month. A city-within-a-city, the Rockwell includes a walled complex of a half dozen thirty-story condo and office buildings, shops, multiple swimming pools, a park, and innumerable amenities. There is ample security: it is a self-contained world, but a gated one, where guards monitor your comings and goings. Once I entered an elevator at 6:30 a.m. on my way for morning coffee when a voice from the security monitor on the ceiling intoned: "Good morning, Mr. Brubaker, good to see you."

"Good to hear you," I replied. "Everyone else is still sleeping." As I said, security is superb at the Rockwell. The same might be said for the housekeeping staff, who keep the marble corridors, sculptures, and paintings dusted and polished daily. There are no surprises here at the Rockwell and the residents like that just fine.

My daughter-in-law Kristen says, "Yes, we live life in a bubble, but it is a very nice bubble." With a twenty-month-old child (whose favorite words are *iPad*, *Starbucks*, and *mango shake*), she values the safety and myriad activities for kids at the Rockwell. She, like her neighbors, has an all-arounder, a Filipina who washes the dishes and the clothes, cleans, provides some child care, runs errands, and minds the cats full-time for about $300 a month. This is substantially above the going rate of $200 because Kristen and my son Andrew feel that $300 is closer to a living wage.

As a former Peace Corps volunteer in the Philippines, Andrew has seen his share of poverty up close, unlike many of his neighbors. While living in a small town in Cavite Province, he got used to "dip and pour" showers and a steady diet of mung beans, rice, and mangos—it wasn't so many years ago. He'd gotten used to waiting in line for twenty minutes just to make a call at the town's lone pay phone. He once ate so many mangos that he turned orange and ended up hospitalized for a week. He was conflicted about his circumstances in Ternate and vowed to help wherever he could. To a large extent, he's kept his promise to give back.

After leaving the Peace Corps, Andrew became part of the Asian Development Bank, a position which pays two-thirds of his rent. He and Kristen are considering hiring a full-time driver, to better navigate the clogged Manila streets in their subsidized Ford Escape. (Judging from the parking lot under the Rockwell, most residents favor more expensive cars, particularly BMWs, Lexuses, and exotic sports cars.) At first, Kristen and Andrew resisted the idea of hiring a full-time helper, but found as foreigners they were expected to do so. The local culture doesn't view this as exploitative; rather, it is viewed as providing a much-needed job that helps to support a poor family. I wondered about this, but thought that it was reasonable under the circumstances. There is a thin line between help and exploitation, and it is easy to rationalize one's choices.

They tell me that the Rockwell is a diverse place, home to all sorts of people. Of course there is one commonality to the residents here: they all have plenty of money. Or at least they have an employer who will subsidize their rent. In truth, the Rockwell is a mix of truly wealthy Filipinos (who tend to keep to themselves) and educated expats from around the world who work at one of the embassies, or at Asian corporate headquarters for firms like Nestlé, Johnson & Johnson, Deutsche Bank, and Volkswagen, or for organizations like the European Union. Others work for international nongovernmental organizations specializing in the amelioration of poverty. Often there is good money in poverty.

There's incongruity at the Rockwell—it is home to intelligence operatives from an odd collection of countries, an assortment of white-collar criminals, and discreetly hidden underworld activities.

In early 2014, Joseph Sigelman, the former co-CEO of PetroTiger Ltd. and a resident of the ritzy Rizal Building at the Rockwell, was apprehended by INTERPOL. He appeared at US federal court in Camden, New Jersey, but was released on $4.4 million bail, on charges of bribery and taking kickbacks from Ecopetrol SA, Columbia's state-owned oil company. He was also hit with conspiracy to commit wire fraud, a violation of the Federal Corrupt Practices Act, and a money-laundering scheme known as the "Manila Split," valued at $39 million. His case is pending, although the company's general counsel has copped a plea. Many shenanigans go down at the Rockwell. For some, it's a good place to hide out.

Folks here tend to spend a lot of time at the Power Plant Mall, and why not? The mall has a six-screen cinema featuring new American releases, a host of fine restaurants, bookstores, upscale boutiques with designer clothes, and a huge grocery store catering to international tastes. You can go to church or have an orthopedist look at your foot. You could live your entire life within its confines.

One might not suspect while living at the Rockwell that Manila is a megalopolis of nearly twenty million people, most of them desperately poor. But as soon as you drive off of the premises, an army of barefooted street kids in ragged jeans and T-shirts will bang on your car windows, begging for coins and food. They are practiced in the art of looking pathetic, though once your car passes they'll be laughing again.

I inquired about life past the Wall, and a number of residents spoke about colorful, vibrant ethnic communities that should not be missed, while others cautioned me about the dangers. One night, I decided to venture beyond this barrier of security, joined by Andrew's friend, an international sustainable development expert named Tito, a Portuguese citizen with an anthropological bent who knew the neighborhood well, surprisingly well. "Believe me, David, I'll show you a building that will stretch your mind," he said. "Let's take a walk."

We met on a Wednesday evening at 9 p.m., waved to the guard, and were escorted across the street by a policeman. I had no idea what I was going to see, but I was intrigued. We navigated our way through a complex of Rockwell buildings and parks, ending up near one of the entrances. Then we turned right.

Unlike the brightly lit streets to which we were accustomed, here was a world of shadows and haze. We saw folks scrounging through trash cans and old men escorted by young women, furtively heading off into the filmy night. The fragrance of tropical plants and fruit mixed comfortably with the stench of urine and fried pork. We were in sensory overload in a place where even cracks in a concrete wall might contain orchids.

Soon we passed a series of dirty restaurants and a few decidedly upscale eateries, one still a favorite haunt of Imelda Marcos. We entered an impoverished Korean neighborhood where a few of the houses looked like they were on the edge of collapse, but most appeared unassuming but functional. Occasionally, a modern, expensive-looking house materialized, but everywhere the locals were dressed in smartly frayed clothes, just hanging out, just killing time, greeting us as we passed by. We never once felt threatened, despite the panhandlers and often overly friendly residents.

We walked through a couple of blocks of girly bars and cheap restaurants wedged between generic hotels. Then we reached our destination, the lady-dwarf-oil-wrestling bar, only to find it shuttered. I asked a man sitting out front in a plastic chair, "Why are you closed?" He muttered, pointing across the street. There, in a little pocket park, I saw a religious shrine complete with a permanent statue of an expressionless Mary and a stern-looking, although temporary, Jesus. Tomorrow would be Easter and preparations were being made. We'd have to wait until our next trip to see the wrestlers—and the midget boxers.

We returned to the Rockwell by a different, more circuitous route, but one not without its compensations. Tito had more to show me. Amid the usual hangers-on and sari-sari stores, we came to one of the largest funeral homes and crematoria in the Republic of the Philippines.

The Loyola Chapel looked like an old motel, and it was huge. Inside, we found a dozen grieving families in what looked like retired hotel rooms, decorated in vintage 1970s Holiday Inn-style. Every room contained a casket with a corpse, with guests sitting at tables eating donuts and commiserating with one another, catching up on the latest gossip. The door to each room featured a picture of the deceased and a bio. From one of these we learned that Conrado "Bo-Bo" Cortez was born in 1925, and that he had been an exemplary mechanic and esteemed member of the local Rotary Club. He was, the bio said, a devoted father and a pretty good basketball player for his age.

The facility could handle fifty viewings simultaneously; afterward loved ones could view the cremation in a private room furnished with a group of chairs and an oven. The ashes were placed in a cardboard box or decorative urn, depending on the plan selected. Owned by Loyola Chapels and Crematory Services, with operations throughout the country, the facility offered a variety of "convenient and affordable mortuary-specific memorial service packages." That is, prepaid installment plans. At this mortuary, the "white package," offered for a forty-three-year-old man, would cost about two hundred dollars per year for five years and would include all arrangements and a standard white casket. No need to bother your relatives with making and paying for funeral arrangements. Pre-planning is not only thoughtful, it's practical.

The McDonaldization of death? Perhaps. Yet in a city so large, with most folks so poor, it offered solace to anguished families. We left the facility not only depressed but in admiration of people so practical, so accepting of death—and so realistic about handling the arrangements.

When we returned to the Rockwell, we were welcomed by bright lights, security, denizens dining alfresco, and a bustling Starbucks. We smiled. We had been beyond the Wall. I wondered which side was preferable.

Bolo-Bolo

I was anxious. Twice I had returned stateside from China to face my overgrown lawn with a vintage push mower. Twice I had developed splitting headaches and nausea and needed to lie down. My physician guessed exhaustion and jet lag, although he thought I might possibly be suffering from an aneurism. I entered the Perlman Center for Advanced Medicine at the University of Pennsylvania, heading to the radiology department for an MRI of my brain. I tried hard to convince myself that it was nothing, but couldn't quite manage it.

As I sat in a hospital gown in the waiting area reading the *Philadelphia Inquirer*, a pleasant technician called my name. She did not convey alarm: "Mr. Brubaker, follow me."

I lay down on the machine's metal shelf and was pushed into the modernistic-looking tube with a plastic cage around my head. I didn't have claustrophobia, but the confinement was uncomfortable. I reassured myself that they wouldn't just leave me in there with another patient waiting, it would be too costly. They'd want me out as soon as possible. Wouldn't they?

"How about some music?" the technician asked, adjusting the headset.

"Sure, jazz," I said. Once the music started, I began to relax. Being in the MRI machine is something of a mind game. It's not the time to think about being buried alive; it's an opportunity to figure out math problems or plan a future vacation. It's a psychological challenge. Then came forty minutes of jackhammer- banging, interrupted only by an injection of contrast fluid midway. After the procedure, I was led back to the waiting room, and the technician said she'd be with me shortly. "Shortly" took a while.

"We need to contact your doctor before you can leave," she said, unsmiling.

"Doctor? Do I have an aneurism? Is there a problem?"

"You don't have an aneurism, but you'll need to speak with your doctor, David Horowitz, before you can leave. We're trying to get him on the phone."

"Well, good luck, he's in Rome."

Five minutes later she returned. I was to speak with a Dr. Woodson.

"Mr. Brubaker, you have a meningioma, do you know what that is?"

"It's a tumor on the surface of the brain, isn't it?" I replied. I wasn't entirely sure—my neuroanatomy was a little rusty.

She explained to me that this growth in the meninges covering my brain was in a good spot, probably benign, but "not small." She added, "You know, a good number of people have these without even knowing it, and most people never have any problems. Still, these lesions can grow, in which case you'll need surgery. You'll need another scan in a few months to see if there's any change."

"Otherwise, I can do as I please? I'm leaving for Rome in a couple of days, is that okay?"

"Yes, but you'll need to see Dr. Horowitz, and probably a neurosurgeon, when you get back."

Twenty-four hours later, I read the radiologist's report. I was worried. Not only did I have a growth, there were numerous problems with my sinuses. What could I do? Brain surgery entails major risk, and I wouldn't want to wake up as someone else.

I began to research my condition. Nothing could be done except to wait for the next MRI, to seek treatment if symptoms developed. This concerned me, because if the tumor grew I could have seizures, memory loss, and other nasty eventualities. Was the tumor new and growing, or had it been there for years, maybe decades?

We left for Rome, just missing the H-man there, and made an appointment with him for the day after our return.

"These types of tumors are usually uneventful, usually so slow growing that patients die *with* them, not *of* them. But you never know. You should have another MRI in a few months, and in the interim it wouldn't hurt to consult with a neurosurgeon," he said. A couple of weeks later, the surgeon said much the same: to him this was a relatively easy case, should surgery be necessary. In the world of neurosurgery, this was a "gimme." But to me…Well, I didn't want anyone cutting around my brain. It's a little too close to home.

Three months later, my wife and I were in the midst of preparing a trip to the Philippines and were looking for a new island to explore. One with a beach. Out of curiosity, I began to research both "Philippines" and "healing," discovering the island of Siquijor, a place with white and black magic, a place of sorcery and healing. Perfect! An interesting venue with beaches, and the possibility of a magical solution to my problem. I remembered that when I once had a sinus infection in China, I'd found numerous remedies that helped me, some of them better than Western medicine. I was both skeptical and open to new approaches.

My research revealed a variety of magical treatments on the island, most of which I couldn't fathom. But I was intrigued by one practice: *Bolo-Bolo*, a noninvasive approach used by witches and faith healers to cleanse the affected area of a person's body, freeing it from disease. The concept fascinated me. Bolo-Bolo employed water, herbal remedies, and incantations. I figured it wouldn't hurt me. What the hell, I thought, why not give it a try? At worst, we'll have an adventure; at best…

I began researching Bolo-Bolo in earnest and discovered that the preeminent practitioner of this art was Nang Conching, an eighty-seven-year-old healer who lived up in the hills in the middle of the island. Marilyn thought Bolo-Bolo wouldn't help but that Siquijor sounded like a great getaway. "Thousands of people swear by Bolo-Bolo, who am I to judge?" I said. We made our preparations.

I can't say that I wasn't warned. Most of the locals in Manila cautioned me not to go to Siquijor, with its black magic, monsters, and strange disappearances. They told me that it was simply too dangerous, especially for a foreigner, although some said that in dire circumstances the magic was powerful and might be curative. I promptly booked our flight to Dumaguete, capital of Negros Oriental in the southernmost part of the Visayas, the closest airport to Siquijor.

Arriving in this picturesque yet coarsely textured city, we boarded an archaic World War II-era ferry that would take us to Siquijor in forty minutes. The boat was crowded with local folks returning with their purchases from the city—there weren't many outsiders going to the island. Nothing seemed amiss—it was simply the Old Philippines, still in place in 2011.

The islanders grappled with their bundles of food and building supplies. Good humored, they were poor and tired in the midday heat. Mothers with unruly children writhed their way into the few available seats in the swaying, perspiring, enclosed passenger area of the boat. Old men smiled and gazed, laughed and chatted. Most folks simply stared out the foggy, translucent windows, eyes fixed on the beauty of the sea, and the occasional pod of dolphins, lost in thought. Some fashionable young ladies sweated and wilted in their finery, while most of the folks were dressed for practical comfort.

I wondered what we were getting ourselves into…On the surface Siquijor appeared to be just another offbeat Philippine island, but it had a reputation. Was the place really dangerous? Would we actually find Nang Conching? And what if we did?

The dock was also vintage World War II-era and as languid as the boat, but we disembarked without incident, turned right over the bridge, and headed for Siquijor Town, the hub of the island and the capital of the third-smallest province in the Philippines. The folks seemed friendly but some smiled at us in a peculiar way, with mischievous grins. I felt a presence about them I couldn't quite understand. I sensed they were harboring secrets, holding something back when I spoke with them. They knew things that we didn't know. Was I imagining all of this? Were my fear and paranoia taking over?

You can buy love potions in the town, and I was tempted to make a purchase. We wandered around town, and I spoke with one vendor, asking her, "Does this stuff really work?"

"Lots of people say that it works, that it works just fine. I have an older man who comes in here once a week, and he swears that it works. This potion has been sold for a hundred years. I guess you'll just have to try it," she said.

We both laughed, she with a twinkle in her eye.

"How many would you like?"

"I'll have one of those small vials," I said, although I thought the price was steep at nearly eight dollars.

Marilyn was not impressed. She examined the small glass bottle capped only with a loose cork and filled with amber fluid and herbs, not only doubting the value of the concoction, but thinking it might be harmful.

In the coming days I would scour the island for the optimal distillates of passion and redemption and picked up a potion for my sinuses. Marilyn was a funkily practical woman, who, dubious but more or less open minded about magic, was more inclined toward Extra Strength Bengay and warm milk.

Perhaps the "menthol, pain-relieving gel" applied to her back would increase her appetite for the balm of endearment, not to mention a better night's sleep. In any event, later I applied the elixir to her lower back.

"What is that stuff?" she said. "It smells really bad. You've got to wash it off."

"Wash it off! It's the elixir of love and it cost eight dollars," I said. "I can't smell anything."

"We don't need this…let me see it," she said pointing to the vial. "Who knows what's in it? It could be dangerous."

"It's not dangerous," I said. "It's an herbal remedy from a healer."

"I don't think so," she said.

Unfortunately, the elixir of love failed to meet my expectations. Inquisitive and adventurous, Marilyn was more sensory than I was. She was drawn to the exotic plants and unusual tropical fruit, but was, regrettably, resistant to the herbal mixtures of healers. Or, perhaps, the potion was a placebo. Still, one must believe…

I kept the potion and have it today. Sometimes I apply some surreptitiously. Marilyn doesn't seem to know the difference.

We had a look around town with its sound but wayworn structures, its atmosphere of comfortable poverty—all accented by allusions to the occult. Medicinal herbs and magical libations shared counters with Coke Light and San Miguel, and vegetable stands sheltered the diabolical in a room upstairs.

The colors of the myriad vegetation mixed readily with the brightly painted buildings around town. The incessant movement of the small, sometimes homemade, vehicles overloaded the senses. Women washed clothes in the polluted river, while their husbands cast lines into the pristine waters of the Sea of Mindanao and throngs of small, eager children teased exhausted dogs resting in the shade. In the midst of the searing heat, people moved slowly.

The market was crowded with fruit sellers and people finding shelter from the tropical heat. The prices looked good to us, but to locals food was costly. Tolerable destitution ruled the island, but I got the feeling that the place was not what it seemed—there were those smiles. I wasn't sure if the joke was on us, or if we were entering a dark place that we didn't understand.

Almost everyone spoke English, except for some of the elderly, who kept to their native dialect of Cebuano. We asked numerous locals about the powers of the witches. Does the healing really work? Some nodded with a wink, indicating, yes, of course it works. Others were devout in their belief and gave examples of members of their families being cured. "But you must believe" was a common mantra. I couldn't believe, exactly, but I could suspend disbelief.

Many said that it was the island itself that had healing powers. Others cautioned us to avoid the *aswangs*—a combination of vampire and werewolf. We spoke with an American woman who'd seen one of these creatures, a ghostlike figure moving rapidly in the shadows. We investigated the island, including the healing waters of Capilay Spring in San Juan, just up the road, and the four-hundred-year-old Enchanted Balete tree said to harbor magical cures. We toured Saint Rita Church and had a look at the well-worn statue of Saint Rita, with her bulging eyes, holding a skull and an upside-down cross. We didn't feel the power.

I began asking people how we might find Nang, hoping that

she was still alive and performing Bolo-Bolo. Yes, several local people said, Nang was still alive and practicing Bolo-Bolo up in the hills, an arduous journey. She had once traveled widely to practice her craft, before age had taken its toll. Once she'd traveled hundreds of miles to perform Bolo-Bolo, to Cebu and Davao. She became famous, but she didn't live for fame or money. She was called by the Deity to practice her craft. Now she was frail and in poor health, but she was still the ultimate healer.

I asked Marilyn what she thought the odds were of my being cured by one of the faith healers. She laughed. "One-half percent chance." In this case, I put the odds at 15 percent. This was an interesting discussion to have with Marilyn, whom I've always called Mary Poppins. Yet she took a somewhat dismissive, if bemused, position toward the dark crafts, while I, the ultimate realist, contemptuous of religion, usually put the odds at one in seven. Perhaps we believe what we want to believe, what we *need* to believe, independent of the evidence. Perhaps there are realities which we simply cannot comprehend.

We asked around and finally found a local driver to take us upcountry to see Nang. He told us that she was famous but now was nearing the end of her life. Like the other "real" healers, she did not charge a fee but did accept donations. I asked what the average donation might be and was told one hundred pesos (just over two dollars).

We entered the Toyota van and the three of us began our expedition. Our driver appeared to be in his mid-twenties, a native Siquijoran, who knew the idiosyncrasies of every road, every turn. It took only about half an hour for him to navigate the narrow mountain dirt road.

Periodically, we passed a settlement, and families waved to us, chickens clucked and pecked, unleashed dogs barked. These were poor people, but they got by with very little. The locals grew a variety of crops on small plots, raised fighting cocks, and picked up day jobs where they could, often at a local resort, which was adding a new building and an additional swimming pool.

Given the communal style of life and the bright sunshine, what we saw didn't look half bad. Folks here looked after one another, and crime was rare, partially because of the fear of repercussions in the form of black magic. Some families lived in separate homes, while others shared—they helped each other to get by. If you harmed me, I or a member of my family would seek magical revenge. It went unstated, but magic underpinned the culture.

The driver turned left into a clearing, into a family homestead, two wooden buildings connected by a small porch. The house was surrounded by brush for a hundred yards and trees grew out front. The encampment was littered with old tires, rusting metal, and sequestered fighting cocks, chained to their perches, imprisoned in wire cages. The requisite canines were out back near a small kennel—as far from the house as possible. Marilyn was apprehensive, but our driver encouraged us not to jump to premature conclusions about the power of this place. I was optimistic, yet my enthusiasm was tempered by rationality, Western-style.

The first structure was actually a sari-sari store, which I supposed catered to Nang's visitors; one could purchase a Coca-Cola, and we did, served by a member of her family, probably her granddaughter. We leaned on a warped wooden fence, enjoying our beverages and the landscape. It took several minutes for Nang's son to see us waiting there, but when he did he motioned to us to come around to the left side of the house, to the veranda.

The building was painted brown and weathered, but it appeared structurally sound. It was rustic, but not too different from structures I'd seen in rural America. On the side of the store, torn posters advertising Jackpot and Champion cigarettes papered the walls. We walked from the store to the front of the house, where we sat on the veranda's attached wooden benches and peered into the one-room, clearly multigenerational home. We saw a large mat on the floor, where everyone was watching a Filipino television channel. They glanced at us as we waited, but found their program more interesting. They had seen this real-life pageant before.

Nang arrived on the veranda from the living room of the house, closing the door behind her. She was not more than five feet tall, hunched over, and very frail. She wore a bright smock of floral design, colorful coral necklaces and bracelets, four rings, and a slight, enigmatic smile. Her demeanor was friendly, but she kept just a bit of professional distance. Her bronzed and weathered skin was still relatively smooth for a woman of her age, and she exuded the regal air of someone who knew many secrets. Not speaking much English, she gestured to ask where I had a problem. I pointed to my head, thinking what the heck, maybe she could cure my sinus problems, too.

Nang Conching, celebrated witch, carried her toolbox with her: an orange plastic bucket filled with water, a clear drinking glass, a towel, a bamboo stick to be used as a straw, a small bottle of oil, and *the magic stone*.

The stone itself looked like any other smooth black stone, but according to her son, in the past, when she'd thrown it into the jungle, it had reappeared the next day on her doorstep. She'd found the stone when she was a child, and for years she continued to throw it into the jungle, always with the same result. Each morning it returned to her door. She did this many times before deciding that this stone was special. She was being called by the Deity to perform Bolo-Bolo, a practice she'd developed over many years. Through trial and error, she found what worked.

In preparation for the cleansing, she arranged her tools in a ritualistic way, as she had many times when practicing Bolo-Bolo. Inspecting each item as she placed it on a wooden bench, she sometimes stopped to clean an instrument or give it extra scrutiny. Nang poured the water into a glass. She repeatedly took the reed and blew into the water, and each time the water became contaminated with a filmy black substance. She ritualistically tossed the increasingly clear water over the railing, blowing and refilling until the water was completely clear. It took about ten tries for her to purify the water. Now the time was ripe for the treatment to begin.

She had me sit on a wooden chair in the center of the porch so she would have room to work. The healing would require her to walk around me several times, chanting conjurations. She placed the magic ink-black stone into the glass and filled it with water. She inserted the bamboo into the water and circled my head with the glass, blowing into the straw as she did so, creating bubbles and a gurgling sound. Apparently, it was important that the glass make physical contact with my head. No area was left untouched. Quickly, the water turned black. Each time she completed a pass, she emptied the glass and refilled it with clean water. She repeated the process several times, and with each successive run over my head, the amount of filmy material, the sickness, diminished, until the water was clear. She then opened a small greenish vial of what looked like herbs mixed with oil and gently poured some of the solution into her right palm. With her left hand, she dipped her fingers into the oil and dabbed my forehead, rubbing it in. I could not discern an odor, but Marilyn thought that it smelled like lavender.

Nang began to whisper incantations while she circled me, chants which I could not understand, probably a blend of the Latin Mass and indigenous paeans. She repeated the process, again and again. She nodded to me that the treatment had been successful and turned toward my wife.

I didn't feel any different after the treatment than I had before. Still, there was something about being in the presence of this woman…Was her sorcery real? I wasn't sure. But there was no doubt in my mind that *Nang* believed in the healing power of Bolo-Bolo.

Marilyn said her back could use some healing so Nang applied the same procedures that she'd used on my head to her back. In Marilyn's case, the process was more difficult, because the Bolo-Bolo required bending and stooping. Nang performed this task silently and with difficulty, but with success. Marilyn felt a twinge of guilt in asking the frail, elderly woman to exert herself, but Nang seemed to enjoy her labors.

Marilyn's session took considerably longer than mine, as the healer performed her ritual up and down her back with many repetitions. We were now "clear." The door to the house opened and her extended family emerged, more animated than before. I handed her five hundred pesos. She and her family were clearly pleased. We gratefully thanked her, summoned our driver, and headed back.

We wondered what would become of Nang's family once the healer died. Some speculated that one of her granddaughters would take over the Bolo-Bolo, but according to our driver, the younger woman did not have the necessary skills or the requisite insight. "You see," he said, "one must possess the powers."

Marilyn remained skeptical about Bolo-Bolo, and said she didn't feel any better after the healing than she did before. I thought that my sinuses felt a little better. Our driver cautioned patience—sometimes the magic could take weeks or even months to work: sometimes the results were not readily apparent.

Shortly after returning home, I found myself back inside the MRI tube, plastic cage and all. With Brazilian jazz playing on the headset, I wasn't entirely uncomfortable. Twenty-four hours later I received the radiologist's report: there was marked improvement of my sinuses, but the meningioma was unchanged. A week later, I met with David Horowitz at the University of Pennsylvania. Half-seriously, I told him about my visit with the old lady.

"Damn," I said, "it didn't work."

His reply surprised me. "How do you know it didn't work? Maybe you would be worse without Bolo-Bolo," he said seriously, but with a faint smile. "And maybe the cure will take more time. Besides," he said, "you can't prove a negative."

The truth is, I don't know. Maybe someday I'll find out.

Morning In Makati

When we were on vacation in Manila, Marilyn had her strategies for getting my arthritic ass out of bed in the morning. She would open the mini blinds, allowing the tropical sunlight to permeate the room, and then say, "Oh, you can keep sleeping, no need to get up." I always got the message.

This morning, as usual, I dragged my aching body to my pile of clothes, dressed, and headed for the living room. I inquired if anyone had figured out how to fix the coffeemaker. They had not.

Andrew had left for work a couple of hours earlier, and Marilyn, my daughter-in-law Kristen, and my grandson Roman were getting ready to leave for a birthday party. I walked to the balcony overlooking the pool and saw it was going to be an excellent day at the Rockwell, warm and sunny.

"Dave, your shoes. Shoes off in the house!" Two-year-old Roman didn't like me breaking the house rules. Born in Rome, he has lived in Makati, Metro Manila, since the age of one month. I imagined a second child would bear the name Manila or, perhaps, Rocky. I slipped off my tropical Vans and handed them to Roman, who promptly ran them over to the pile near the front door.

"Mango shake, Dave?" He knows I'm usually a soft touch.

"Maybe later, Roman. Hey, where's your Buddha-in-a-box?"

Roman headed to another room to retrieve this souvenir of the Hong Kong night market, and, smiling, handed it to me. "Great, very cool! It looks just like Big Buddha, remember him? High on the hill?"

"Yes, Buddha!"

"Where are you guys going?" I asked.

"We have a birthday party for Sameika," Kristen said. "It's an important one, she's two. It's a really big deal. They sent an engraved invitation, just like for a wedding. Fancy schmancy. I've never seen anything like it."

"Are you coming with us?" Marilyn laughingly asked. "We'll probably drive."

"It'll be fun, it's at the Peninsula," Kristen added, smiling or smirking, it was hard to tell.

"God, no. I couldn't bear twenty two-year-olds, especially without coffee. Besides, you know what I think about this…I'll meet you at the Coffee Bean around two o'clock, how's that?" I'm usually grumpy before my coffee.

"Okay," Kristen said, "but we may be a little late, depending on traffic," she added, gathering items for the trip.

"Don't run over any homeless kids. I'll expect you around three. Don't feel that you need to hurry. I'll be fine as long as I have my papers and my coffee. Besides, I need a walk."

I'm a walker; it's when I do my best thinking, and I feel better when I am moving. I slapped on my wayworn Temple University baseball cap, inserted my pipe between my jeans and belt, and looked around the four-bedroom, five-bath condominium for a magazine. Finding a two-week-old copy of the *Economist*, I retrieved my Vans by the door, said goodbye, and was off to feed my morning addictions of nicotine and caffeine followed by a newspaper chaser.

As I waited for the elevator, I studied the Oriental rugs and the tasteful Asian art, while marveling that there are only four condos per floor in this part of the Rockwell. In the lobby, I admired the polished marble, the freshly cut flowers, and the Filipino tapestries, and greeted the doorman and security with a salute, which he returned. They'd encountered me many times and knew that I'm friendly. Still, they didn't seem to know what to make of me. I had to be rich, because I come often, but my bearing sent another message.

Exiting the building, I filled my pipe with a Balkan Sasieni blend, a pungent mix of Macedonian and Latakian tobaccos. Generally this blend cannot be smoked around others, who often describe its aroma as "essence of burning tires," but outside in the breeze the taste was exquisite. As I stood on the top step of the portico, I watched a procession of Land Rovers and Lexuses, with their hired drivers picking up the children of the wealthy for playdates, parties, and school. The children were commonly referred to as "darlings" and the mothers' group as MAD—Mothers and Darlings. These children are investment capital, sent off to the best schools accompanied by their ya-yas, child tenders who run errands before returning to prepare lunch. The mothers wave goodbye after making last-minute adjustments to the darlings' clothes.

Watching them, you might think that these women were the idle rich, a characterization they would find insulting. After all, overseeing large household staffs, shopping, and socializing can be exhausting. While observing their morning ritual, I thought of Thomas Jefferson's adage about the desirability of periodic revolution, thinking the body politic might be in need of a cleansing enema about now.

Before heading out, I noticed a woman in a bright but tasteful floral dress with a nervous smile, waving to her daughter as the driver opened the passenger door of her Mercedes SUV. She was having an affair, according to rumor, with one of the maintenance men, and feared that her husband had grown suspicious. She looked afraid. There are many people like her at the Rockwell.

The mall did not open until eleven, so I decided to take a long walk to the Starbucks around the corner from the Ateneo University Graduate School. This particular Starbucks, one of many in the area, was not crowded and had an outdoor smoking section. Reloading my pipe in the morning sunshine, I greeted dog walkers and their well-dressed charges, several armed guards, and some neighbors whose names escaped me. Starbucks is Starbucks, but it met my needs.

"Hi. I'll have a grande house blend, black, and a plain bagel with nothing on it." Some people drink coffee for its taste, but for me it's nothing more than a caffeine delivery system. I like the taste of coffee, but I drink it as self-medication.

"For here or to go?" asked the barista.

"For the patio."

Waiting for my coffee I glanced at a woman staring at me and smiling. She placed her order and moved closer.

"Where're you from?" she asked.

She was dressed in a stylish blue jogging suit and she winked at me. She must have been sixty, and it was happening again. My God, I thought, I am catnip for codgerettes. I didn't want to talk with this woman and, in fact, always tried to avoid the kind of coquettish geriatric women I attract. Maybe they make me feel old, maybe they're just bored or lonely, I didn't know. But I didn't want to talk to her or to anyone else. I wanted my caffeine-nicotine-reading fix and nothing more. I needed "Dave time," and I knew I couldn't provide therapy to everyone. Then again, maybe she saw me as a lost soul in need of therapy myself. I'm not the neatest dresser.

"I'm from Pennsylvania, and you?" I tried for polite.

"I'm from Massachusetts," she purred in a rattling kind of way. "So what brings you here? Do you live here at the Rockwell?" See reminded me of the women who ask if I'm a famous director or inquire about my pipe.

"I'm just visiting. I'm here for caffeine."

"How do you like the Philippines?" she inquired. "Where have you been?"

Just then my order arrived. Fortunately, because I had ordered black coffee, it arrived quickly, while hers was a more complex concoction. I grabbed my goodies, said goodbye, and headed for a small table with an awning just around the corner and out of sight. I waved, not wanting to be curt, "See ya." I'm not alone in my peculiarities; most tables were filled with individuals reading newspapers or working on their computers. Starbucks sells solitude, not just coffee.

After the requisite refills, my fog began to lift. The mall would be opening by now. I entered it on the second floor, walked past the Maserati on display, and took the escalator to the fourth floor where I entered Fully Booked. I headed to the newspaper section and purchased copies of the *International Herald Tribune, Philippine Daily Inquirer, Malaya Business Insight* and *Business World*, all for 180 pesos, just under $4. I walked across the corridor to the Coffee Bean and Tea Leaf, where I ordered a large Columbian, black, and sat down to read. At precisely three o'clock, they appeared.

"Hi Dave, mango shake?"

"Sure, Roman, let's get one. I need coffee, too. How was the party?"

"Good, look at my new book," he said, holding it in the air.

"Nice, I like geography books and so will you. *The World Around Us*. Great. We'll have to check out all the places that you've been."

"Kristen says she needs a skinny latte," says Marilyn. "Are you up for another coffee? I'd like a cherry blossom tea…"

"Of course," I say, wondering what a skinny latte might be. "Did you have fun?"

"It was good," Marilyn says, "but noisy. There were twenty-four toddlers, at least one ya-ya apiece, sometimes two, plus the mothers and only one father. He left as soon as he could. I can't blame him: it was chaos. It was held in a ballroom, they had techno music and the kids were getting tired. How was your day?"

"About usual," I replied.

Morning in Makati

Santo Niño

My two-year-old grandson Roman is an American citizen, although he was born in Rome and moved to Manila at the age of one month. He is a tropical boy, distinctly fair-haired and vanilla in a land of many hues, and he has adapted well to his surroundings. He sweats as easily as he smiles, and at the Rockwell he is a celebrity. He especially adores and is adored by the younger ladies, the ones who wear suits or uniforms and whose heels click on the marble floors of this affluent enclave. They like his light skin, his energy, and his blond, curly hair.

Some parents look for dolls that resemble their children. In Roman's case, he is the spitting image of the national icon—the statue of Santo Niño of Cebu, said to have miraculous powers. Santo Niño is a figurine of the Christ Child and was a baptismal gift from Portugal to Queen Juana of the Philippines in 1521, delivered by the explorer Ferdinand Magellan to cement an alliance between the two countries.

Santo Niño has proven to have enduring virtues. He received the papal blessing of Pope Paul VI in 1965 and Pope John Paul II in 1981. You can buy replicas of Santo Niño in any mall and in many of the small stands found throughout the country. Images of him are ubiquitous. You'll see him in pizza joints, at the ice cream parlor, and in many taxis.

Made in Belgium, Santo Niño looks much like the Infant of

Prague with his bright red adornments, gold crown, and light skin; he's encased in bulletproof glass in the Basilica Minore del Santo Niño in Cebu. Many tales exist of the statue's supernatural powers, when it was stolen and found its way home without human intervention, or when it was cast into a fire but did not burn. The third Sunday in January is Santo Niño's feast day in Cebu, and I wonder what would happen if Roman attended the event.

Understandably, Roman is the subject of considerable curiosity and even adoration from the country's Roman Catholic population. He is a luminary in the Philippines. Locals like to take his picture and touch him. He has, until recently, endured his burden magnanimously, but now he is growing less receptive to the constant intrusion. He has taken to showing his displeasure by saying "Go away" or a firm "No" or putting his hand up to signal "Stop!" This is problematic for his parents, who have taught him to be friendly and kind, but his patience has begun to wane. It isn't fun anymore—it is irritating. Like other two-year-olds, Roman doesn't like to be harassed.

But his admirers show no mercy, and while most don't actually believe him to be the reincarnation of Jesus, others aren't so sure. Why take a chance? It might be wise to get a picture with the child or at least *of* the child. It would be even better to touch him, as one might touch a holy relic, perhaps by asking for a high five. Sometimes folks literally grab Roman from his mother's arms, to hold him, kiss him, and photograph him. This can be disturbing.

Personally, I have never witnessed any of Roman's alleged extraordinary powers.

Roman's appeal no doubt emanates from his very light skin, treasured in the Philippines by a population enamored with whiteness. Half of all Filipinos buy skin-whitening products, making it perhaps the world's largest market next to India. There are creams and sprays for all parts of the body, and some claim to have the additional benefit of retarding the aging process. I have never heard anyone in the Philippines discuss the relationship of white skin and, for example, melanoma. Skin cancer isn't a concern. Better to use whitening products and stay out of the sun.

Light skin has been good for Roman, who has already been featured in advertisements for organic toy cleaners, a hotel, and a shopping mall; I've often said that perhaps he could make a living as a spokesman for baby and toddler products if he acted quickly.

Two-year-olds bear many burdens, but being likened to Jesus is rare and especially difficult. Recently, we took a vacation with Roman to Boracay, in the Visayas, the heart of Santo Niño-land. Boracay boasts one of the best beaches in the world, and I was in need of sandy rest. But getting to the beach fifty meters away proved to be a major challenge. Within a day the employees at the hotel all knew Roman, and they wanted to touch him. Cameras were sometimes surreptitiously pointed in his direction, but just as often they were pressed just a few inches from his face.

"Touch baby," "High five," "Give me a kiss" became screeches to me, an irritating encroachment on my seclusion. Even in the surf the harassment continued. When a Chinese woman grabbed Roman from his mother so a friend could hold him, he understandably became testy.

Women were his most aggressive and devoted admirers, and they were not all Filipino. Women from Korean tour groups were particularly drawn to his charms, Catholic or not. The large contingent of Russians in Boracay ignored Roman, however, as did most men, except for the young male hotel workers.

One evening we went to dinner at a small, crowded Greek place featuring flaming dishes and boiling soup. His mother held him on her lap as he ate. As I glanced around, I heard a scream as Roman inadvertently thrust his hand into a bowl of scalding soup, requiring a trip to the emergency room to treat his second-degree burns. They demanded a number of medications, and he suffered. He screamed for hours as his parents tried to comfort him, and, later, put him to bed. I was hopeful that he would recover quickly, while fearful that he would be hurting for several days.

But the next morning Roman was back to his old self, his hand and arm largely recovered. Despite the blisters, he was seemingly happy, playful, and unusually cooperative—eagerly smiling for the cameras and joking with the hotel staff, guests, and other admirers. In fact, he became animated and seemed to feed off the previously unwanted attention. It was as though his accident had never happened; it made me think of Santo Niño.

You can't be certain about Roman, I thought, what the hell. I held up one hand.

"Roman! How about a high five?"

With his good hand he complied, with a giggle and an admonition: "No more soup, Dave. It burns."

Tony

She looked out from the pastry counter, a stylish woman fondling a tomato. The caption read "You say tomato, I say fuck you." A refrigerator magnet, she had many friends, including a smiling Jesus, proclaiming "Jesus loves you, everyone else thinks you're an asshole," and a 1950s-vintage woman saying "I'm not really a bitch. I just play one in your life." I was standing in the checkout line at the Dosie Dough bakery in Lititz in the heart of Pennsylvania Dutch Country, and I wondered who here would buy these magnets. Lost in thought, I heard a familiar voice from the back of the store.

"Dave! Dave! I need to ask you for a favor." It was Stanley.

"It depends on what it is," I shouted, indicating that I'd meet him out front. I paid for my Diet Coke and *Philadelphia Inquirer* and was soon joined on the patio by a smiling Stanley, sandwich in hand.

There's an unreality about the Dough (home of the "Best Buns in Town"), a retro coffee and sandwich shop, the gathering place for the town's glitterati, or, some would say, eccentrics. In addition to town folks seeking a drink or taking a break, there's always a man working the crowd, looking for a job. Another man, a retired airline pilot, lurks to hit on women. He prefers the ones who are married, because they are often available, create "less hassle," and "are easier to get rid of." Then there's the old guys' table, a bunch of conservative Republicans who spend every morning bitching about the current state of affairs. A few of them appear to be confused and out of place. Sometimes it is hard to tell them apart; they ramble on in much the same manner about current events. They like things the way they used to be.

You hear foreign tongues at the Dough, too. Others wait for their appointments around the corner at the Christian tattoo shop or the psychiatrist's office across the street. One man who used to come here ran for mayor and worked as the town's Santa at Christmas. He had his picture on the bulletin board inside the store, but it was taken down when he was sentenced to eight to fourteen for molesting a thirteen-year-old girl and sending hundreds of solicitations to other girls online. The Dough is filled with hipsters, hucksters, and visionaries, and everyone has a story. It's pretty cool. I take an anthropological interest in the local fauna, and I enjoy the comedy and pathos of their biodiversity. Sorting truth from fiction is no easy task at the Dough.

And then there is Stanley, a jolly retired social worker with creaky knees and a heart condition, looking for love in all the wrong places. At sixty-six, he has a twenty-two-year-old wife and is a rock star to the town's old guys. Their wives are less enthusiastic.

"When do you leave for Manila?" Stanley asked.

"We're leaving on Sunday for a month," I said.

"Can you deliver some money for me?"

"Now that depends. How much are we talking about, Stanley?"

"Two hundred dollars."

"No problem. Who do I give it to?"

"A guy named Tony. I met him during my last visit to Manila. I want you to give him a hundred for himself and hundred for his daughter, Nina. So she can stay in school. Tell him he can use his money for whatever he wants, but you've gotta emphasize that the other hundred is for his daughter, Nina, and strictly for school expenses. I'm half-afraid he'll pocket it all, and Nina won't be able to go to school without it. She's fourteen. She's at a delicate age."

"So just who is this guy?"

"Oh, he's a tour guide. Strictly word-of-mouth. He introduced me to my wife, Peaches. I owe him," Stanley says.

Stanley felt sorry for Tony, said that Tony's living conditions weren't the best: "I slept there once and never will again. Every time someone gets into bed someone else falls out."

He added that I might find Tony's place interesting, but that it's hard to find, suggesting that I meet Tony near his home in Quezon City, maybe at Robinson's Galleria in Ortigas. Stanley handed me the two hundred and a slip of paper with a telephone number written on it and repeated what I was to say to Tony. "That's a lot of money in the Philippines," he said.

"Hello, Tony? This is Dave Brubaker, a friend of Stanley."

"David! I have been waiting for your call. Stanley told me about you. He's a great friend, and we've had some wild times together." My mind conjured up a 255-pound Stanley dancing naked on a table. When he gets going, he's capable of such things; he loves hanging out nude on Orient Beach in St. Martin. The vision is laughable to me, but if he's enjoying himself, why not? What's the harm?

I suggested we meet at the Coffee Bean, over at Robinson's. I explained that the Bean was near the Asian Development Bank, where we planned to meet my son Andrew at four o'clock. Tony lit up when I mentioned ADB, and we agreed to meet at two. He was quite familiar with Robinson's.

"I'll see you there. I'll be wearing a baseball cap and a

Hawaiian shirt," I said.

"Don't worry, I'll find you," Tony said.

When Marilyn and I arrived at the Coffee Bean, Tony was waiting for us. I handed the money to him and repeated Stanley's instructions. Tony struck me as odd, in a used-car salesman kind of way. Effusive and smiling, he was a little too friendly. He wore a baseball cap that brayed "Groundhog Innovation" and a T-shirt proclaiming "Provoke. Hold Hands Shyly," whatever that might mean. His eyes darted around the mall, as if someone might be following him.

He was a man in a hurry who liked to talk in an endless cascade of words. He laughed easily and answered our questions about the Philippines with candor. In his hat, with his smooth skin and slight frame, he was a man whose age was difficult to judge, but his nervous excitement was palpable. He was hyperanimated and smooth, with a Miss America smile. After a little chitchat, I asked him about himself.

"I'm a freelance guide, strictly private customers. I like to help people. I introduced Stanley to Peaches and urged her to go with him. I think the match is a good one. She never finished school, but she's a hard worker and will help him. He's not in the best of health. How are they doing?"

I told Tony that after a couple of months spent searching for a job, Peaches now worked long hours at a local business, and that otherwise she seldom left their apartment near the Dough, preferring to stay home and Skype her family in Cebu or watch horror movies on Filipino TV. I didn't tell him that she avoids the sun because she wants to become as light skinned as possible to impress the folks back home. Or that Peaches can't make change very well. But she's an excellent shopper, with a preference for expensive clothes, particularly Versace and Coach. She adores Victoria's Secret.

We decided to sit there a while to get to know Tony.

"David, you need to understand. Stanley wasn't a sex tourist.

He isn't well and for him it is the idea of a young girl that's fascinating. He wants companionship and someone to help him as he declines. You really can't blame him, can you?" As Tony spoke, I could read Marilyn's mind. She found the conversation fascinating but repugnant. Her cringe was barely concealed.

Tony asked if Peaches is sending money home, because her family desperately needed help. "They are very poor and Stanley is paying their rent and buying things for them, like a refrigerator, a computer, and aircon. He is paying their electric bill, which is important because otherwise the appliances would sit unused. He's considering buying property and building a house for his old age outside of Cebu."

"I think she is sending money home, but I know that Stanley wires them a check every month and when they need something extra, which is often. He cares about the people he meets. You know, Stanley is especially concerned about Nina. He wants a better life for her," I said.

"As do I, my friend. She is very beautiful." He took out his wallet and showed us his daughter's picture, just a kid. "The money will help her stay in school. She is fourteen, but she needs to buy uniforms and supplies, pay jeepney fares, and so on. Without school, she'd just hang around and get into trouble."

"What would *she* like to become?" Marilyn asked.

"Actually, I am trying to introduce her to foreign gentlemen. She needs someone to support her, because I can't. A retired Australian man has shown interest. This would be the best thing that could happen for her. I hope things work out. We'll see. In the meantime, school, thanks to Stanley."

"You'd really give your daughter to a foreign guy? How old is he? What would *she* like?" Marilyn asked.

Tony said that the Australian was the ideal age, around sixty-five. And he had money. Tony said girls in the Philippines often have no future, because life is expensive and marketable skills are usually impossible to obtain. A retired foreigner can transform the lives of these girls and their families. Americans, Germans, and Australians—they're all here.

"This shocks you, but you need to think about where you are." Tony smiled. "These men mean a better life, sending money home. So what if the girls are fourteen? David, the men get companionship and the girls get security. I'm Nina's father. I want her to have a better life. Don't you see?" Tony was smiling, but he was clearly frustrated. He could tell that Marilyn knew this would be a good deal—for Tony.

He told us that he'd placed lots of girls. He admitted arranging matches was an inexact science and that he'd had some failures, like the time that he'd fixed up a sixty-five-year-old man who had hidden boils over much of his body with a fourteen-year-old girl. The man turned out to be eighty and very sick with little money. They moved to Cebu, but the man died, and Tony ended up paying the girl's way back to Manila. She got nothing from the match. Sometimes older foreign men exploit young girls, making empty promises.

"He looked great for his age," Tony said. "David, I've gotten a lot better at this over the years. Few people fool me now. I can weed out the sadists and the scammers." He looked confident.

Marilyn kicked me under the table. "There must be a better way," she said. "Would a foreigner help Nina get an education? That's what she needs."

"Perhaps, but in reality this seldom happens. We must live in the real world. You should visit my place. You'd see, you'd understand," he said. Marilyn interrupted saying we had to be at ADB by four o'clock.

"Maybe next time, Tony. We'll allow time to make the trip… What kind of tours do you give?" she asked.

"I show people whatever they want to see in Manila. I'm at your service," he said with a snide smile.

"How did you meet Stanley? He seems to know you well," I said.

"I met Stanley on a website called Filipino Kisses. It matches older men with Filipinas. I help these gentlemen to make the arrangements. Many of these men fantasize about the Philippines and these girls, and I show them what is real and what is not and help them to navigate the culture." The money Tony earned from this service helped him sustain himself, and he freely admitted he couldn't survive without it. But he seemed to relish his job. The cash from Stanley would help, he said, because there were eight people living in his small hovel: his two daughters; his two sons; his girlfriend Sugar, a refugee from the pineapple fields; and two girls from his hometown of Siargao whom he was trying to place. Tony seemed relatively educated, quite bright and yet…

"Before we leave, how about a picture?" Marilyn said, and we stopped a passerby to take it. She wanted something to prove to Stanley that we'd actually met Tony. It was an odd request, I thought.

Later that evening, Marilyn and I discussed our meeting with Tony. She was appalled, not only because he was earning his living by trafficking young girls, but that he intended to sell his own daughter. He was open about his business, even discussed his business plan, as if he were selling vacuum cleaners.

"He supports all of these other girls, why not his own daughter? He could provide for her if he wanted to," she said, "easily. Why doesn't he just become a real tour guide—he certainly knows the area."

"To Tony, the kid is expendable, a financial drain and an irritation. He said she was born in Mozambique. Who knows if she's really his daughter anyway," I said. I felt Tony was without a conscience, morality just didn't factor in. He was totally pragmatic. I was surprised that someone hadn't killed him long since. Then again, it's a question of survival, both for the girls and for him.

Marilyn said, "This is all so wrong—and criminal. And what about Stanley?" she asked. "He was a social worker!"

I stuck up for Stanley. He had many good qualities. Once, he'd spent a month scouring yard sales for baseball gloves to hand out to needy kids in the Dominican Republic. All he knew was that they played a lot of baseball there and were very poor. The man was generous. He'd been all over the world and was always eager to share his knowledge—and his money. He was a tired and lonely man who loved the sunshine and vivacious young girls. In Lititz he failed to attract local women his own age or any age. And he probably only had a few years left, if that. If he and Peaches were happy, where's the harm?

I said, "Stanley is in denial. He just doesn't see the age of the girls as an issue. To him it's just a matter of taste. Yeah, the idea that Stanley is helping these girls by sending money is a rationalization, but you can't deny the depth of the poverty in the Philippines. There are lots of things in this world that I don't like—I've seen far worse in rural China. We do what we can and live as best we can. He knows that some of these girls are scamming him, but he doesn't seem to care. He sees himself as helping them."

Marilyn smiled at me balefully, unconvinced.

"You know my father served in World War II in the Philippines. I grew up on his tales of wonderful, beautiful people in a tropical paradise, and I promised him that one day I'd go there. That's how it started," Stanley said on my return. "We often talked about the Philippines, but he never returned." We were back on the patio of the Dough. "Thanks for delivering the money. How'd you like Tony?"

"Well, we had a pretty odd conversation. He was very open

and friendly…but kind of strange, a little nervous."

"Oh, that's Tony. He comes off as untrustworthy, but I can tell you this: he usually keeps his word. And he's fun to be around, and God he knows everyone. You really need someone like Tony to help you through the maze." He explained that sometimes girls sit all day in Internet cafés, hoping to scam men for money. They agree to meet these men, but say they need money for airline tickets or new clothes, or maybe for a deposit at a hotel. Most of them don't show up. "I sent cash, lingerie from Victoria's Secret, and other gifts many times. I learned my lesson: a foreigner needs help," he said.

"He's a 'tour guide'? I'm not sure that's the right description," I said.

"After a year of back and forth with him online, I joined him in Manila for one of his tours. He said that he'd show me around the volcano, which he did. He also showed me what you might call the underbelly of Manila. He's an amazing guy. During the summer of 2011, I was staying at a five-star hotel down by the US embassy. We met in the lobby one night and Tony suggested we go out. He took me to a spot called the Cowboy Grill. The place was huge and packed. I made some new friends there. Tony had talent and he had great dance moves. A little bit gay, but an unbelievable dancer. Of course, many of the acts were guys in drag. It took me a while to realize that. As the evening progressed, things got crazier and crazier. I loved it there."

"A little bit gay?"

"Straight, gay, it doesn't matter to Tony. He is whatever the situation requires."

"What about his girlfriend, Sugar?"

"Tony's from Siargao, down south, very poor. Sugar's parents gave her to Tony to take to Manila to make arrangements for her. At the time she was fifteen, and, you know, eighteen, nineteen is over the hill in that world. They couldn't even feed her. She was my vision of a Filipina, a chocolate dream, beautiful."

"Eighteen is over the hill?"

"Absolutely. The foreign market, these men, are looking for fourteen- or fifteen-year-olds, not older. Except some older guys want a wife with an RN to have someone to care for them in their old age. Still, even nurses can't be over twenty-five. After that they too have problems attracting men. I don't like it, but that's how it is."

"Stanley, why isn't Tony in jail?"

Stanley explained that the age of consent in the Philippines used to be twelve, but in the past few years they'd raised it to eighteen. "You might say Tony is involved in trafficking, but he'd say he's providing shelter and security for the needy, that he's providing advice only. Maybe it's in the eye of the beholder. You should see where he lives; it's like *Slumdog Millionaire*, only worse. Believe me, I know, I've slept there. It's not only hot, it's hell," Stanley sighed, "and now his new girlfriend, a twelve-year-old, is pregnant."

"What happens to these kids? When they're older, where do they end up?"

He said that the boys usually find work abroad. "Most have no skills and work as day laborers. Those with skills do a little better. The girls dream of becoming nurses and moving to places like the US but few do. The nursing schools are expensive and demanding, so it's tough to make it through."

I told Stanley that I used to work at Johns Hopkins, which had many Filipino nurses. They earned good money, so there was plenty for them to send home to help out.

"Yes, in a case like that the family feels like it has won the lottery. The odds are about the same."

"And the others?"

"If they don't find placements, working in the malls is a possibility up to the age of twenty-five. If they aren't married by then their best shot is to try to latch onto a foreigner, a difficult proposition at that age. They mostly work as caretakers or ya-

yas. Or as prostitutes."

"I need another coffee, I'll be right back," I said. I reentered the Dough to confront a new display of magnets. One caught my eye: a smiling woman saying, "Want a kid? Take mine."

Lucky Buggers

In my travels around Manila I'd often heard vague references to a "Lucky Buggers Club," and the concept fascinated me. "Lucky buggers," as it turns out, were the male "trailing spouses" of expat wives. Largely from Europe, New Zealand, Australia, and North America, these women had taken good jobs in the city, usually at places like Johnson & Johnson or the Asian Development Bank. They came to Manila for exceptional job opportunities, including high salaries, rent subsidies that enabled them to live in exclusive condominiums, and a slew of discounts and retirement goodies long gone from jobs in their native countries. Usually these jobs were difficult to obtain, intellectually stimulating positions with substantial responsibility but reasonable hours. The working conditions were excellent and there were many fringe benefits: free dental care, subsidized tuition for their children. Their colleagues were a bright group of adventurous and well-educated expats, and they all traveled widely, often to nearby Asian locations, sometimes only an hour or two away.

How many people have been to Papua New Guinea or Tajikistan? The husbands of these women, so I'd been told, had, while living lives of luxury, playing golf, watching TV, and hanging out in wine bars at upscale malls. There was little incentive for them to work, especially at low-low Philippine salaries. This sounded like a dream to me, the opportunity to live one's life free from worry, with the resources to pursue whatever was of interest. We'd all like such freedom, wouldn't we? I set out to find these men.

"I haven't come across anyone like that here," said Tito, a suave, thoughtful, and relaxed forty-something Portuguese whose wife worked at ADB. "I have never met a character like this. There are playboys, guys who latch onto women with money, but even they are rare." Tito himself was an expert on sustainable development who worked off and on for organizations like the UN Development Program and the World Bank. He was a full-time doctoral student at the University of London, writing his dissertation on the impact of climate change on poor people, and until recently he'd handily earned more money than his spouse.

"My wife's job has been great for me," he said as we surveyed the Makati skyline one evening from his spacious thirtieth-floor condo. "I can study for my PhD while continuing to work part-time on projects that interest me. It's only fair. Now it's *my* time to explore my passions."

"No one does *nothing*," he insisted. "What woman would want to stay married to a man who drinks and watches TV all day? These are smart women who wouldn't be interested in dull, parasitic men. It isn't real, this Lucky Buggers Club. It's a fantasy. Personally, I need to keep learning, keep exploring. I'd go nuts watching TV all day. My God! I need challenge and stimulation," he said, adding, "I'm experimenting with new things like pottery and photography. Manila has an amazing art scene."

Tito had befriended a well-known Manila artist and collected his work, displaying a number of the man's paintings in his apartment. He had also enlarged his collection of antique furniture; over the year he had developed an eye for a bargain. Tito had a taste for the good life, but was busy…very busy. "I don't have time to waste," he said.

He was a fine photographer, specializing in portraits of street people, and was both a wine connoisseur and an epicure. While he was an expert with respect to chocolate and other goodies, he was also kindhearted, a man who had rescued two street cats and donated generously to charities to help street kids. He did what he could, where he could. I liked him—he was a very bright guy, thoughtful and kind.

Still, Tito didn't help me much in looking for lucky buggers. I scoured the area for signs of the club and soon hit pay dirt. The Lucky Buggers Club, Philippines, actually existed, at least online, helping its seventy-plus members to "socialize through sporting activities (golf, diving, bowling, etc.) and lunch…we have actually been known to volunteer our time to charity or other social projects as well. We try to stay out of trouble by keeping ourselves busy with, well just about anything we like really, and just as long as we don't get our better halves too angry with us (a little angry is okay)." The club also claimed to foster the "nourishment of our minds" through "criticizing world politics and politicians." As one might expect, the club kept a low profile. It invited readers to have a look at its members-only Facebook page, suggesting that "while you're at it, check out the Lucky Buggers Golf Club group." The club had recently, for example, sponsored an archery contest at the newly opened Ortigas Center. The group was not simply about "drinks, fun and games," but also about charity. After all, they'd painted a schoolroom in Tondo.

The membership included traditional lucky buggers, a smattering of retirees, and the merely wealthy, but membership requests had to be approved by a committee. The requirements? At least partial residence in the Philippines and a wife who works full-time or who had inherited a substantial cache, although being retired or independently wealthy was just fine. Members were allowed to work part-time, although many did not—the practice was discouraged.

I scrutinized the group's Facebook page, looking for

information. There was little public information available because I wasn't a member of this closed group, but it seemed to be legit. I sent a membership request, but to no avail. I posted a request for information. Nothing. They seemed a little secretive, and they were not interested in my candidacy. Still, the group appeared to be real but attracted members by word of mouth. I wanted to learn more.

Ensconced at the Rockwell, I asked Andrew and Kristen if they could identify some lucky buggers for me. "I don't know anyone here who fits the description," Andrew said. "Everyone 'does something,' whether it is taking care of children, working part-time, going to school, or starting a business. Looks can be deceiving: the guy you see reading at the pool every day could be a student or he could be trading stocks. Your club, I think, is a myth."

"Do you really think so? They have a Facebook page," I said.

"The only club around here is the Rockwell Club, and it has a helluva lot of activities, including a giant state-of-the-art gym. God, half of the people who live here are there in the morning working out, and I've never met any of your lucky buggers. I've never met any at Forbes Park or Global City either. Even the ones you might expect to fit the description are doing business or reading. Some of them make deals while running on the treadmill. These guys don't just sit around. Nobody would do that, especially in the tropics and in a place offering so much…" Andrew, tanned and toned, a weekend bicycle enthusiast with a twelve-thousand-dollar Italian bike, seemed slightly annoyed by my line of questioning. "Well, there probably *are* such people, but I've never met one."

Kristen added, "It's true…everyone is busy with something. I don't think that anyone sits around drinking beer and watching TV, except maybe Alphonso, and he's relatively new here. He's always over at the Brewery, you know. Sampling their 160 kinds of beer from all over the world. He's there, except in the morning, when he goes to Starbucks and reads the papers and socializes. He's very open and likes to talk to the locals. You should talk to him." Kristen spends her time at the yoga studio and in the gym, painting, and works for the Rockwell by giving art lessons to other residents. She is also active in Mothers and Darlings, where she serves as an officer. This organization attracts mothers and their children for group activities and is a way for new arrivals to meet other expats. "God, it's a lot of work," she says. A side benefit of MAD is that it sponsors family activities, bringing together fathers who often know each other from work or the gym.

Undeterred, I spoke with a number of expat men, such as Diego from Portugal, a short, thin man who was about forty with a mischievous smile and a goatee. Most of the time I wasn't sure if he was putting me on, because he'd make a statement and then laugh. Despite having a full-time ya-ya, he was a hands-on father for his two kids, aged two and six months, with another on the way. "Kids are only young once and they need guidance. You cannot delegate this responsibility!" he said with a stern chuckle.

A lawyer by training, he indicated that the employment situation in Portugal was "terrible" and his wife's job a godsend. When I first met him six months earlier he'd described the Rockwell as "a kind of upscale ghetto," but now his opinion had changed. "It's pretty nice here, I can't complain," he said as he motioned toward his ya-ya to collect the toys. Was he a lucky bugger? I wasn't convinced, but thought he was getting close.

While relaxing at the pool I met Kristen and Andrew's friend Tim, an American early retiree. Though only in his thirties, he'd scored big in Silicon Valley. His Dutch wife worked at Nestlé. A large, pudgy man with a boisterous personality, he said, "I'm going to see if I can find some consulting work once I am more established. But I'm in no hurry." He spent his time managing his investments, reading, arguing politics with his neighbors, visiting the pool, and traveling with his wife. He was from Wisconsin and a graduate of the Ohio State University. A sports addict, he frequented a sports bars to watch the Minnesota Vikings and Ohio State Buckeyes in the middle of the night.

A lucky bugger? He was new, but a promising candidate. I thought I'd check back with him in six months. Childless, with household help, his responsibilities were minimal. And I noticed that he liked to talk about sports, business, and the latest movies. He was a right-winger, and he loved telling me about how climate change was a liberal myth and that Obama was going to destroy America. I wondered if he was joshing me, or if he believed what he was saying. I noticed that I often couldn't tell when near lucky buggers were being serious. He had a nervous smirk and never missed his weekly massage, which was performed in his condo.

Craig, an Australian, and his wife, Turquoise, a Gabonese, had worked for almost a decade for NGOs in countries such as the Gambia and Togo, helping street kids. "You know," Craig said, "the agencies in Manila have, until recently, been old school, loaded with men. That is changing rapidly, and this place is Valhalla for well-educated women of color. They receive hiring preference, and what with Turquoise's master's degree in economics from Cambridge…" Stooped over, friendly, and in need of a shave, he loved sitting at the pool and reading or simply staring into the cloudless sky. Slurping a watermelon shake, he seemed exhausted. While he must have been in his early forties, he looked considerably older. He didn't look well.

"What are *you* up to?" I asked.

"I love the Rockwell. The four years before we moved here, we both worked for a Catholic NGO in Bangladesh, which was very difficult. Our living conditions were harsh, and our work was sometimes dangerous. As non-Muslims, we had cultural restrictions—lots of things that we couldn't do, like drink, and we ended up staying inside in the evenings. It was tough. So for now it's strictly R&R for me, but I do hope to get on with an NGO here in Manila. With my wife working at ADB, money, for once, isn't an issue." It was premature to think of Craig as a lucky bugger, although he could evolve into one. I thought I'd keep an eye on him.

Darren was an American teacher who had married a wealthy Malaysian woman and moved to the Rockwell when she was appointed to manage her family's timber business in the Philippines. "I went to a crappy, bottom-tier school, and I wasn't much of a teacher," he said, "and for now, I'm happy to get out of the grind and enjoy myself. Someday I might help with the business. Quite simply, we're fortunate to have money. I love my wife, and the freedom to do as I please is great."

Darren, in his late thirties, appeared to be in excellent shape. He paid strict attention to his appearance, which was slightly formal and very neat. He said he was busy most days with playgroups and going to the gym. He often went with his three-year-old son to the Rockwell Park with a group of ya-yas and their charges, and, as the only male in the party, was a favorite—several of the ladies had a crush on him. He seemed to relish his role as a sex symbol. He was unusually open and engaging and I felt that I was getting closer to lucky bugger-land.

What about expat women? I thought. Maybe they were the real lucky buggers, even if they were ineligible to formally join the club. "Well, I can tell you this," Tito said, "with the household help, some come close. Some women love flamenco dancing or watercolor and that's what they do all day."

Some women had multiple helpers, so there was plenty of free time: their main responsibility seemed to be managing the helpers. The Rockwell was a good place to raise children, and for many women with kids the schedule looked like this: the ya-ya or the all-arounder would take the child to preschool, then there was lunch and a nap at home and a party or playdate. The mother could be involved as much or as little as she liked.

There was plenty of time for yoga or art classes, and some took advantage of their good fortune. Free time meant opportunity. She could go to school or start a business, while still guiding her children's growth. It was hard to beat, although some complained constantly about how busy they were and how difficult it was to fit everything in. Some initially resisted hiring helpers but later found them to be an essential part of living in Manila, where mundane chores like getting the car fixed or shopping for groceries can be major hassles. It took time to integrate into the milieu. It was a process.

As for the men, I came around to Tito's view: everyone seemed to be doing something. I did not find a single person who simply watched TV or drank all day, although there may be a few such people hidden from view, within the confines of their luxury condos. Rather, I saw people doing what I would be doing in similar circumstances: enjoying life, while trying to figure out how to be productive and happy in a strange new environment. Lucky buggers? Hell, they were all lucky buggers, even the ones who worked, though some won't realize it until they return to their home countries and to harsher realities.

And my search made me see that I, too, was a lucky bugger, spending my time uncovering the truth about lucky-buggerdom, learning from people who were living the dream of freedom, free from financial worries, time constraints, and the coarsening cultures of their home countries. While they lived in a bubble, they had freedom to exploit their talents that their friends back home would envy. If they wanted to pursue a business opportunity there was a network to help them. Everyone knew everyone in this world-within-a-world, and life was good. With so many well-placed friends, strings could be cut. Who wouldn't seize such an opportunity?

I applied again for membership in the Lucky Buggers Club, the organization that was not supposed to exist, explaining my unique situation as a lucky bugger writing about lucky buggers, and that I was a frequent visitor to the Philippines. I also mentioned that I stay at the Rockwell. This time my application was accepted, and I joined the fellowship of mostly Philippine-based buggers—trailing spouses, retirees, and the wealthy, and was encouraged to attend club events whenever possible.

I can hardly wait for the Christmas party.

All-Arounders

"Pick it up," six-year-old William screeched, "pick it up right now!" His helper, a Filipino woman in her late twenties, looked at the ball he had just dropped. He was testing her, throwing his weight around. She shrugged and complied. After all, she needed the job, and some mothers are quick to replace all-arounders. Some even have a "no bruise" policy, meaning that if a child comes home with a bruise the all-around woman is fired. I thought this absurd and counterproductive. What kind of adults would these kids grow into? How do all-arounders do it? How do these women cope?

Visiting Manila on a regular basis, I became interested in the lives of the all-arounders, the women who unobtrusively performed most of the household chores. Almost every affluent family employed one. They were always smiling, and I wondered what their lives might be like. What did they really think about working for the wealthy in a city with endemic poverty? What was behind those smiles?

They intrigued me, and I began to talk to these women, in conversations that went beyond the customary perfunctory greetings. I noticed that most all-arounders were anxious to talk but also were fearful of the prying ears of their employers. I met with several of these women privately, assuring them of confidentiality and that in my writing I'd mask their identities.

Like me, they were interlopers in the world of the wealthy, and I wanted to learn more.

Lemon's eyes told her story. Almond shaped and brown, they were at once inquisitive, anxious, and depressed, belying her nervous grin. She often seemed on the verge of tears, even when she smiled, which was often. She surveyed the restaurant as if it were a foreign land, reminding me of Iron Eyes Cody, the Native American actor who'd shed a single tear for a despoiled landscape in the "Keep America Beautiful" commercials of the 1970s. As with Mr. Cody, a tear said it all.

Lemon seemed eager to tell me more of her history and was at once exhilarated and intimidated by the midscale Italian place in which we were having dinner. Such a restaurant was a rare treat for her, where a decent meal might cost a week's salary. Yes, of course, I said, she could order what she pleased, and shyly she ordered her first glass of wine. Her eyes darted around the room, as if she were afraid someone might see her. She was clearly worried. Maybe having dinner with a sixty-five-year-old American would look bad. She seemed hungry to please, but almost frantic about her situation, and she repeatedly referred to her advancing age at thirty-nine as an impediment to future employment and her ability to buy food and pay the rent—to survive.

She was short, perhaps a tad overweight, and wore braces on her teeth, an anomaly for workers in her situation. I considered asking her about them but didn't. She had aspirations, and she knew deep down that she could be more than an all-arounder. Lemon seemed bright and articulate, too educated for basic household labor.

Lemon would be a good teacher if given half a chance— she could be *somebody*. The oppressive poverty in which she found herself had taken a psychological toll, although with the exception of a general sadness and edginess, she appeared healthy. I wondered about her composure—she seemed to be working hard to keep herself together, and she had a number of nervous tics, such as reflexively smiling when spoken to. The fear in her eyes, the anxiety in her voice, and the compulsion in her demeanor seemed to have resulted from a life of chronic deprivation, precariousness on the margins of society. Her movements were jerky and she was in constant motion—especially her eyes. She did enjoy a good laugh about life's absurdities, and said that she was smarter than many of her employers. She probably was. I got the feeling that she was also on the edge of a breakdown, delicately trying to balance relationships, logistics, and finances.

I had met Lemon at a children's party at the Rockwell and initiated a conversation. I had inquired about all-arounders and the lives they led, and was introduced to her by a friend of a friend whom she worked for occasionally. I wondered how a bright, energetic woman had come to be working as a household helper. She was eager to talk and wanted me to understand her situation. She'd wanted to tell me privately, so I suggested dinner and she immediately accepted. She clearly wanted to share her travails with someone from outside of her world, someone she could confide in. Or perhaps she was simply looking for a good meal.

Lemon lived in a one-hundred-square-foot room with four other people—a couple with a small child, and her sister, Apple, who worked off and on for a number of families and was frequently changing jobs. Apple's pay was low, but she always had a few pesos; she knew how to maximize opportunities. She had found the room at a decent price. She knew people.

There was no kitchen, but a small bathroom was attached to the main room. This was a major improvement from Lemon's previous living situation, a somewhat smaller room with a bathroom down the hall in a building populated by prostitutes and petty criminals, in a neighborhood where an evening stroll might lead to tragedy.

Lemon and Apple's room was in a newer, well-constructed, safer building in an ever-so-slowly gentrifying neighborhood in Makati. Lemon didn't quite appreciate the changes underway but her room was closer to work and to potential new opportunities.

In her world, Lemon was a success story. Unlike most other women in her position, she had persevered to obtain education and contacts, and she earned money enough not only to survive but to improve her circumstances. She wasn't living on the street or in homemade slum housing. She might not be able to afford a snack at the Dutch Bread Hauz, but at least she lived close by the place. She could see the freshly baked goods from the street, and she could dream about tomorrow.

Instead of taking three separate rides to get to work—which could take more than an hour—she could now walk in less than ten minutes. Maybe she'd lose a little weight if she could avoid those cheap little donut shops around Matilde Street. The rent was higher now, but she had no transportation costs and more time. She could earn a little extra money on the side, tutoring children in English, or babysitting. She was self-sufficient, unusual for a single woman of her age, with her life history. She was also a lifelong resident of Manila, and she had avoided the overwhelmingly polluted and destitute slums of the city.

Working for an American couple with a small child, Lemon was an all-arounder. She did it all, as the name suggests, for about two hundred dollars per month. Working for a relatively undemanding family permitted Lemon time to earn extra money in the evenings or on Sunday. Some all-arounders worked twelve-hour days, making it difficult to earn money by moonlighting. These were usually "live-ins" and could save on rent, but at the cost of being available to the family twenty-four hours a day.

"If you are an all-arounder here, you are nothing. I am worried about my future. I must work hard while I'm still young enough. Most employers won't accept you if you are above thirty-five, and I am thirty-nine. Most women my age work at sari-sari stores or clean the streets," she said.

"But you work in an upscale area, doesn't that help?" I thought she might make some good contacts and impress the "high ones."

"We are usually not even considered people, although there are exceptions. I have to accept my situation since I have no choice. I am saving to buy a small house so I can survive when I get older. I have no one, no parents, only my sister. If you are old and sick, without help, you will become homeless and die. If I could find a job abroad I'd do it, but my age is a problem. Getting married and having a family is not a priority. I have to support myself."

Lemon and her sister Apple had been orphaned when their parents were killed in an automobile accident. The sisters went to live with their grandparents, poor people with three other kids to care for. Her grandfather worked as a car mechanic until he lost his arm in a chipping machine, forcing the girls into an orphanage operated by the Daughters of Charity. Lemon was then eleven, Apple nine.

"I was lucky and I learned to be diligent. Here it's survival of the fittest. You want to save yourself. I studied hard to build a future for myself," she said.

"How were you lucky?" I asked.

"The nuns found a sponsor for me. I graduated from National Teachers College with a degree in psychology. I had a partial scholarship, but I had to work five hours a day to earn money while going to school. I ate noodles, dried fish, and canned goods for four years. I couldn't afford rice, because it was too expensive. It is ironic that rice, vegetables, and fruit are abundant here, yet they are too expensive for most people. Mangos are almost four dollars a kilo! How could I afford a mango making nine dollars a day?" Like many Filipinas, her finances and her taste buds had driven her to cheap fatty and sugary fare, which, in truth, she now preferred.

"Can you market your degree? That certainly sets you apart from the other all-arounders, doesn't it?"

"I am hoping that I can find a job in a school. I've done some tutoring, and I hope that this will eventually be a way out. The degree doesn't mean much, but I'm thankful that God helped me. I should have studied nursing. Something more practical."

I wondered about the other fifty or so girls at the orphanage, about what might have happened to them. I asked her about them.

"Most could not find sponsors and were on their own at sixteen. Few options existed for them. Some became helpers, others became prostitutes. In any event, there are no legal protections for them. Being an all-arounder can be hard work, and some girls are just lazy. You can earn more money as a prostitute and work fewer hours. Some are lured into it by phony advertisements in Manila, but others come willingly."

"Isn't it dangerous?"

"Mr. David, of course it is dangerous. Most of them get sick and some are killed. The safest avenue is to work as a live-in all-arounder to rich foreigners. Americans are best."

"Why?" I asked.

"Americans pay better and are more generous. They are less likely to treat you like an object. That's been my experience. Many people treat us like shit. One Chinese lady I worked for often said, 'Come little monkey, hurry.' What could I do? Americans will not treat you this way, and they usually pay better and give you more time off. Unfortunately, there aren't enough Americans to go around," she said with a sorrowful laugh.

"It sounds like you've worked for many families."

"Yes, Mr. David," she said, recounting the dozen or so employers she'd had. "Usually foreigners come to Manila for a few years and then move on. Each time they leave, I need to find a new job. Working in a wealthy community has helped, and as long as I have good references I can find another family. You know, expats often sell or give away furniture and clothing when they leave. That's where I get most of my clothes. Don't tell anyone," she said with a twinkle. "One woman I worked for gave me all her old clothes. She'd worn them only a few times, so I dressed very well in those days." I admired her persistence and cleverness but wondered about her frequent job changes.

Lemon ordered some chocolate cake for dessert. "It's so big! Do you think that they'd let me take some home?" It turned out that Lemon loved desserts as much as Italian food: she didn't need a doggy bag.

"Sure. How about an after-dinner drink?"

"I'd like that," she said, ordering another glass of wine. "Mr. David, I really appreciate this."

"What's up for tomorrow, Lemon?"

"I'm working from about seven in the morning until five at night. Then I'm serving food at a party over in Ortigas."

I wondered about her future. Lemon worked continuously, had little personal life, and seemed overwhelmed. "When I come back here in six months, will you still be where you are?"

"I hope not, Mr. David. There is a new preschool that has opened just two blocks from where I live, and they are looking for teachers. I have very good references and hope to work there, if they'll hire me full-time. I know some of the families with children who attend the school so I'm hopeful. The pay is about what I am making now but the future is better."

"I am very surviving," said Rosa, an all-arounder working for a family at Makati's upscale Rockwell complex. A small, chunky, vibrant woman in her early thirties, she was proud that her skin was a little lighter than the other all-arounders'. After all, she had worked hard to produce and protect her complexion. She knew which products worked and which didn't, and she knew where to look for deals.

"Many Filipinos have dark skin, from living close to the beach, to the wind and the sand," she said. "I've dedicated myself to having better skin. I buy the best products, and I avoid the sun." Rosa seemed preoccupied with skin tone and spoke of it frequently, almost obsessively. I was concerned about her.

"Why is skin tone so important?" I asked. I had difficulty understanding why people with beautiful, smooth skin would want to bleach it with chemicals. I thought about the cost, about skin cancer, the absurdity.

"Because the best jobs go to lighter-skinned people. That's just the way it is. Lots of products in the stores will lighten your skin. Very safe and contain vitamins."

Rosa lived in Makati, where she has a small rented room to herself. She was friendly and seemingly open, but somehow reserved. Her professional demeanor revealed no emotion. We sat on her employer's veranda, a fantasy for an all-arounder, overlooking an Olympic-size pool and a grove of palm trees. I noticed a visceral stoicism, and she seemed without compassion when we talked about the street kids, the slums. She was a tough customer, and she clearly was strict with the family's children. I wondered if she'd ever considered a career in the military.

Rosa's morning ritual had her arriving at about 7 a.m., changing into a T-shirt and worn jeans, putting her long brown hair into a ponytail, and downing some coffee and a couple of sweets. (I noticed that she loved chocolate and frequently made goodies from raw cocoa beans.) Unlike many employers, her family permitted her to wear street clothes rather than a uniform. At the end of each day, she changed into fashionable clothing and shoes, unfastened her hair, and sprayed on a little perfume. She didn't appear to be an all-arounder. In fact, she looked as though she might be a resident. Rosa bought most of her clothing at charity sales in the affluent Bel-Air development, often paying less than a dollar per item from departing expats. She also favored okay-okay stores, the Filipino equivalent of American thrift stores, which were surprisingly little patronized in Manila. The government limited the importation of used clothing, citing national pride.

"I have only two jeepney rides to get to work, and I work in a high-status building. My dream is to have a small house in my province. This would be good for old age but not for now. In the province there are no jobs. I get back there once a year to visit my four-year-old daughter. I think my parents are raising her the best they can. This is what I must do."

She seemed to have a positive attitude about life. It wasn't an emotional attitude but seemed intellectual and detached. I wondered what my attitude would be if I were in her position.

"You know, my whole family is Christian, but I am a Buddhist. I began attending Buddhist services when I worked for a Japanese family, and it changed my life. Now I'm happy."

"How so?"

"If you've got too much money, you're not happy. I have seen this many times. More important is wisdom, Mr. David. Peace of mind is necessary to obtain happiness, and Karma is my new life. I don't need to blame God or other people. Once you enlighten your mind and change your attitude, you'll feel differently. Catholic teaching is full of blame and shame. Most Filipinos think that you should be thankful to be alive. But I want to be happy." I wondered if Rosa really believed or even understood what she was saying. Her comments seem memorized, and she didn't seem happy.

The Philippines is a Roman Catholic country where there can

be a heavy social penalty for those leaving the faith. There are Buddhist Filipinos, but most of them are of Chinese ancestry. "What does your family say about this?"

"Mr. David, in my family, you must make your own decisions. They respect what I have chosen." She told me that her family in Bohol understands the need for individuals to find a way to survive, as long as they continue to maintain close ties to their families and send money home.

"Tell me about yourself, Rosa. How did you end up here?"

"Mr. David, I am from a small village in Bohol. I have two brothers and two sisters. I was lucky to be able to graduate from high school, but there were no jobs. Our livelihood comes from the sea, and the fish catch has fallen, because of the typhoons and pollution. If you stay in the province you'll have nothing. Most girls leave for Manila or Cebu at about sixteen or seventeen, those remaining marry and have lots of kids. Most of the men are alcoholics and it is getting worse. Fighting and more fighting." I had been to Bohol, a land of pristine beaches and the Chocolate Hills. It was a place of great beauty, a little wealth, and tremendous poverty.

"Most leave at sixteen?" I asked. "That seems awfully young."

"Oh, yes! I wanted more in life. I had to get out, but there was no money for college or anything else. I was in a difficult situation, but very common. I married young, divorced, left my daughter with my parents, and came to Manila. Now I am able to send money home every month. I am very proud. I did this on my own and did not depend on others."

"So it's worked out well for you?" I asked.

"Yes, now. I had a number of jobs that were unpleasant. My first job was with a Chinese-Filipino family, and I worked until one or two in the morning. I lived with them, and they woke me up at all hours. It was a twenty-four-hour-a-day job, and I felt abused and exhausted most of the time. I was paid very little. To tell you the truth, the Chinese want your services, but pay little."

"And your other jobs…?"

"I worked as a saleslady but was only permitted to work until age twenty-five. It was fun, but the pay was also poor—no future for me. Not enough money. I worked at a fast food place washing dishes, but I was allergic to the detergent and they let me go. Then I worked for a Spanish-Filipino family, very nice people but same poor pay. Then I worked for a Japanese-Filipino family. The woman was a concentration camp survivor. They were very strict but fair. They told me about Buddhism and took me to services with them. Buddhism changed my life. I worked for them for nearly three years until they went back to Japan."

I wondered how she saw her future, and I asked her if she planned to stay in Manila indefinitely.

"Oh yes! Last year when I went back to my province, I saw my friends' lives. They are unhappy with more kids, still alcoholic husbands, no jobs, and more fighting, fighting. It's a miserable life, lots of abuse, and my friends are depressed and hopeless. Mr. David, they think that they must embrace their lives and are afraid to go to Manila. I'm luckier than my friends—my life is better here. When I go back to my village each year, I am treated like a celebrity. I bring pictures of myself with many foreigners. I'll bring a picture of the two of us," she said without smiling. Her friends back home envy her lighter skin and urban clothing, she told me, and they wonder about how this was achieved. Her dad often tells her to wear more modest clothing while at home.

"You make Manila sound pretty good," I said.

"There are many problems. Sometimes employers treat you badly and there are no real legal protections. Standards exist, but they are just words that people ignore. People from the provinces are shunned because of their dark skin and because of their dialects and lack of education. But really, I think that education is better in the provinces because the classes are small. Here, it is so crowded. Kids here go to school for only half of the day because there are too many students. It isn't perfect either place. Of course, many girls from my province go to Cebu or elsewhere, maybe half come to Manila. The ones who do not leave are the ones who suffer the most. And, of course, there is the government. Much corruption. Manila is controlled by gangs and syndicates!" Finally, Rosa showed real emotion. "And they give nothing to the people who need help." Employing families often complain that there are too many protections, too much regulation.

"What do the girls do to earn money when they leave the province? I know they are expected to send money home."

"It is harder for the males to find jobs in Manila, but easier for them to go to another country. Mr. David, the girls either work as helpers or in stores, or they get involved in organized crime or prostitution. I have a friend who became a prostitute in a high-class cabaret. Most of the women working there have college degrees. The clients are rich and educated, and they want the girls to be cultured, able to discuss a variety of subjects. She had no education but was hired because she was smart and very beautiful, with skin that was almost white. Now she is wealthy. She married a rich German who sent her to college, and now she manages a sizable business. She has a wonderful life."

"I take it, Rosa, that your friend's experience is an exception?"

"It's sad, but people in my province assume that if you are working in Manila, you're a prostitute. Often, it's true. Some choose prostitution because it is easier than working a regular job. Many Filipinas are lazy. Others have little choice. They, of course, hope to be rescued by a foreigner. I can't blame them. Mr. David, we are trying to survive. I do not question the choices that others make. Sometimes they go to Japan, where the pay is higher. But that is not easy."

"Rosa, you said you'd like to save money and retire back in Bohol. What would you like to do in the meantime?"

"The pay here is very low, even for highly educated professionals. I'd love to work in Hong Kong, Canada, or the

United States. I look around. I study the matter. In the meantime, I go malling with my friends, Videoke. We're happy and we don't forget to laugh. Maybe I'll get lucky and catch a big fish in the cabaret!"

Jo-Jo was excited. After four months of expensive paperwork and language classes, not knowing if her effort would pay off, her visa request had been approved: she would be leaving in a few days for Hong Kong. An all-arounder, she would follow her Japanese family, and for that she had needed that new visa as soon as possible, or she would have lost her job.

We met in the living room of her temporary employer, after I had obtained permission to speak with Jo-Jo at length. There was no one around, and we sat on the ornate teak chairs, looking out at the Makati skyline, at the financial capital of the Philippines.

"I'm leaving because my former boss transferred to Hong Kong. He's Japanese-Chinese. I will have a two-year contract, and then I'll return to Manila and my son. I need to save money for a house here in Manila, for my son's education. The pay is so much better there. The visa process was a struggle because the applications are expensive. I had to go through an agency where it is always money. I needed to pass a physical examination. I have respiratory problems, so I wasn't sure that I'd ever be approved. And I had to study Chinese, which was difficult for me. I had to memorize a great many phrases. But I'm actually going! I actually passed the physical!"

Jo-Jo was leaving her son for a job that paid about $150 a month more than she was presently making. She appeared apprehensive about the move, but leaving her son was not a major concern. I thought about the personal cost of a few pesos, and for an elusively prosperous and tranquil retirement in Batangas. I wondered if she'd ever get there.

"You look healthy to me," I said. Looks can be deceiving, especially in places like Manila, where disease often goes untreated and the pollution levels are high, but Jo-Jo seemed young and healthy for her age.

"I have had years when I was very sick, and I was worried about being certified to go to Hong Kong because of the physical examination. They check you all over, perform many tests. You know, I have had three children and two of them died, one at three months and one at one year. They died of pulmonary problems like mine. The healer in Bohol read my palm and said that none of my children would survive, but she was wrong."

"Have you ever been out of the country?"

"No, but I feel as though I have traveled. I have often gone with my families on vacation, to care for the children. I've been to Boracay, Siargao, and to Cebu. You can find anything in the Philippines: mountains, beaches, cities. Foreigners are just starting to find out about us. To tell you the truth, Mr. David, I am a little nervous about this. I've never been away from my son for more than a week, but I know that my sister will care for him. I'll save money, and we'll have a better life."

"That's a big adjustment for both of you. When will you see him again?"

"The contract says that I can return home for two weeks after one year. My boss is a fine man so maybe it'll be a little sooner. You see, rich people are not all bad. He helps the street kids, he's responsible. And there are others like him. He's always looked out for me."

Jo-Jo seemed animated and warmhearted. With her smooth brown skin and expressive smile, this small woman seemed bigger and younger than she really was. She'd graduated from high school in 1986 and it was now 2013.

"Where are you from, Jo-Jo? Where is home?"

"I am from a village near Batangas, down south, and every year I return to visit. I have a brother and four sisters in Manila, and two sisters and a brother there. We were rice and coffee farmers, but my father is now a teacher. I got married at a young age, but my husband was a terrible alcoholic and so we divorced. My second husband was a good man, but the children's deaths drove us apart. We divorced."

"In the village I worked at a sari-sari store, but after divorcing for a second time, I needed to make a new life for myself and my son. We moved to Manila to live with my sister, and I found work with a Belgian family in Makati. The husband worked at the Asian Development Bank, and his kids were older and went to the International School of Manila. When they moved after six years I found another family. This is what happens to all-arounders working for foreign expats. You never know. I have been with the same family for eight years, and now Hong Kong! I am very proud to be working for this family, and I feel very close to the children. I feel as though I've raised them."

"How is your family in Batangas?"

"My mother is sick with pulmonary problems, and, because of a spine injury, my father just lies around when he isn't working. He will have to stop teaching after this year. I'm always sending money to them. Mr. David, I have to tell you that I've had difficulties with my family. They do not understand that I have limited resources, and my mother, who never cared about me or my health, is very demanding. At least my father has always worked. Bohol is filled with poor people who are lazy and don't want to work. They can't read or write and they don't want to learn. Alcohol is a big problem and the kids suffer. Even with work my family is poor. Before Manila there was no electricity. Water is far. No food. It is different in Manila." Poverty, she explained, is relative.

"But you've made a life for yourself."

"My sister was my savior, and my brothers helped me. My sister works as a ya-ya for a wealthy family, one that has two for only one child. My brothers work in construction whenever they can. We have always worked together, and will again in two years. I never received a peso from my ex-husbands, and I send money home and take care of myself. I have some skill, some knowledge, so I'll be okay."

"Hong Kong is a beautiful and vibrant city. But it is very expensive and chaotic, like Manila. But maybe you'll enjoy it there and stay in Hong Kong longer."

"Oh, no, I will be back in two years. I know that I'll miss my son, and I'll have money to buy a house. The Philippines is a beautiful country, and I would like to get married again."

The extremes of wealth and poverty in the Philippines were, at first, disturbing to me. After a while, I got used to the class system, the deprivation of the many and the opulence of the few. Perhaps it is this fact that is the most disturbing, that we begin to accept the unacceptable, making change that much more difficult.

Lemon, Rosa, and Jo-Jo are thriving, compared to many of their contemporaries. These women work hard, and they endure long, difficult bus rides. Their sometimes temperamental employers can fire them on a whim, and they have no pensions, little job security. For this, they have only enough money to share a small room. With no savings and growing older, they are chronically insecure and a tad paranoid. I can't blame them.

They leave their own children with whoever is available, to care for the children of the wealthy. Often they see their kids only once or twice a year, generally for brief visits. Some are resentful. The waste they see is almost unbearable, and the temptation to steal quite real. They understand that the hardship—living in a polluted environment, poor health care—will shorten their lives. They have no alternatives; still, things could be far worse. They could be living in the province with abusive husbands, no electricity, and little food. They could be on the street. It's all relative.

Joseph

Most people don't know that Central Lithuania was an independent country from 1920 to 1922, or that Danzig, Fiume, and Mozambique Company were countries that once existed but no longer do. I knew these unusual facts when I was thirteen years old, from collecting stamps. This was around 1960, when department stores like Gimbels in Philadelphia had large philatelic departments with not only stamps but the finest Minkus-brand collecting supplies. Mom-and-pop stamp stores dotted the suburbs.

Nowadays, stamp collecting signifies codgerdom, but I persevere. I have collected stamps from the Philippines for fifteen years, making an annual advance deposit with the Central Post Office in Manila. A woman named Lourdes sends me a package every six months, wrapped in cellophane—repurposed underwear packaging—with the latest issues. Now for some unknown reason, Lourdes has left the post office, probably retired, and the stamp service no longer seems to exist. I'm on my own.

And so, one threatening Monday during the rainy season in Manila, I schlepped down to Lopez Street looking for a cab to the main post office. While there, I planned to visit the old walled city, mostly destroyed in World War II but home to an excellent bookstore specializing in odd Filipino topics. It was typhoon season, when the skies often turn dark, almost an obsidian black. So when the clouds blackened, I should have taken the hint, but I didn't. After a few minutes of waving, I made eye contact with a driver.

"Can you take me to the main post office near Intramuros?" I asked. "I'll pay you extra." He sped off before I could even get the door fully closed, not saying a word. I hailed another cab.

"Can you take me to the main post office near Intramuros?" The driver ignored my request and drove off. It took fifteen minutes, and three more attempts, before I got lucky.

A surly-looking cabbie rolled down his window and asked, "Where are you going?"

"I'm going to the main post office near Intramuros, can you take me there?"

"It's far and the traffic is bad today. Many lights. It's a Monday."

I thought things were looking up—difficult but not impossible to convince the cabbie… "I'll give you a good tip!" I said.

"Well, okay. But it will take over an hour. Go ahead, get in."

The sign on the glove compartment said that his name was Joseph, and the musty but new Toyota was covered with debris, as was he. Joseph looked a little like a Filipinoized version of terrorist Khalid Sheikh Mohammed in the infamous mug shot. He appeared to be a man in his fifties, drained of energy, disheveled, frustrated, and a little desperate. He cast his bloodshot eyes in my direction, and I knew I was in for a harangue. Most cab drivers in Manila don't talk much, and if they do they are probably trying to sell you something or take you where you don't want to go, usually for a nefarious reason. Drivers frequently ask lone male passengers if they would like to meet girls.

The dashboard had things pretty well covered for the eternal Joseph, holding a small plastic statue of Santo Niño and one of the Infant of Prague. The Virgin Mary peeked at me from just to the right of the steering wheel, and a small crucifix hung from the rearview mirror. Filthy, the car was strewn with a hundred papers across the front seat, brochures, candy wrappers, and gasoline receipts.

"Do you live around here?" he asked.

"No, I'm just visiting my son. He lives at the Rockwell."

"It's very expensive," he observed.

"It is," I said, "but his employer pays most of his rent."

Navigating the heavy traffic, Joseph stopped at a red light, rolled down his window, and purchased a lone cigarette from one of the *tak-tak* boys who come up to your car selling singles. "Mind if I smoke?"

"No, not at all," I said. I knew full well that smoking was not permitted in taxis, but I didn't want to jeopardize my ride, so I just opened the window. Besides, I was fond of the smell of burning tobacco.

"You know, it is very expensive here for me. I rent this car for thirteen hundred pesos a day, and a liter of gas is fifty-seven. And I have a wife and four children!" he said.

Joseph was working me over pretty well.

"I have a good deal for you. I have a sister who sells condos," he said, opening the glove compartment and retrieving a somewhat bent brochure while narrowly avoiding vehicular homicide. He handed the folder to me. "Here is your new residence."

The brochure described a dozen new condo complexes, all built by the same developer. It read: "Constantly inspired by the spirit of innovation, Avantia introduces a unique portfolio of vibrant neighborhoods, groundbreaking living solutions, and master planned communities that nurture individuals and hard-earned investments with a singular vision: giving you a place for living well."

"How do you like them? I think that you'd like the Solandrica best. Don't just dream…live." If the name sounded made up, that's because it was. The brochure described Solandrica as an "elite environment" where "one can live in a highly coveted community," a place for "Manila's most successful."

"I live in the United States, so I won't be needing a condo," I said, "but they look good."

"How about your son? He could save money by buying a place. It would be a good investment," Joseph said softly but firmly.

"That wouldn't work. He gets a rent subsidy from his employer but would get nothing if he owned a place."

Never at a loss for words, Joseph asked me if I believed in Filipino-American friendship.

"Of course."

"If you buy a condo, you will be contributing to friendship and the Filipino economy," he said.

"But I live in the US," I said.

"You could move here. You'd be helping my family. Good investment. Or you could take vacations here," he implored.

"But I stay with my son when I'm in Manila."

Joseph rifled through a stack of papers on the front seat while stopped for another cigarette. "Ah, here it is. Here is a price list with my sister's information. Call her *today*. She'll give you a good deal." Joseph was starting to snarl. He was running out of time.

The prices were low. With 5 percent down, the monthly payments would be as little as five hundred dollars. Avantia seemed to be selling the appearance of luxury rather than luxury. I suspect if there was a tremor, these buildings might not hold up. I had noticed that cheaply constructed condos for the growing middle class were being thrown up all over town. Many people aspire to the Rockwell, Forbes Park, or Bonifacio Global City, but few have the means. In Forbes, for example, homes run five million dollars and more. Many of the Philippines' wealthiest people live there.

Personally, I prefer the Rockwell, for its location close to the Dutch Bread Hauz and because it was built to withstand the inevitable earthquakes and typhoons. In the Philippines, like much of Asia, developers are often willing to cut corners to save time and money. Some use chemicals that make concrete harden quickly. Unfortunately, it also makes buildings brittle. You do what you have to do.

Joseph's sister, whose card listed a residential address north of Ortigas, would probably earn a year's salary by selling a single unit, and Joseph was relentless. "Look," he said insistently, "this is a one-time opportunity. You can help my family and make a good investment. It will bring you to the city more often."

I didn't respond. He pitched Solandrica for the entire seventy-five-minute ride, and I felt for him. He was doing about all he could to earn money, to keep his family intact. Navigating from the selvage of society isn't easy. I couldn't blame him.

It began to sprinkle as we drew close to our destination, and Joseph, pointing at the post office in the distance, informed me that I'd have to walk the final five blocks due to traffic congestion. The meter said 202 pesos so I handed him 500. I left the car and Joseph exited quickly, screeching his tires in the tropical heat.

The walk helped me to mentally recover, but only for a few minutes; I was about to enter the main post office. I walked up the decaying steps and approached the front door, which was caked with the alluvium of a generation. Maybe more.

I passed through the decrepitly elegant entryway to the security station, seemingly manned by lobotomy survivors. I crossed the artistic but broken tiles and went to the information window.

"Where can I buy commemorative stamps for postcards and collectors?"

Without looking at me, the uniformed attendant pointed right, said, "Window 42."

The building was cavernous, dank and Kafkaesque, and it reminded me of something out of a horror film, or of the old Broad Street Subway in Philadelphia. I went to window 42 and settled into a wait. Finally, I reached the head of the line.

"I'd like ten postcard stamps to the US and a price list for philatelic items."

The clerk said, "Window 13."

At window 13 there was no line, just a young man in a T-shirt and jeans reading a newspaper, from which he was not going to be distracted by a mere customer. I called to him and he said, sarcastically, "Windows 21 and 22."

The thin lady at 22 said, "No, you want 24," pointing "right over there. Lucille will help you." Unfortunately, there was no Lucille and no stamps at window 24.

Eventually, I found the correct window, 39. The friendly, if tired, woman behind the counter slowly prepared my order, and then, laboriously, began affixing the stamps to the post cards—three stamps each. "Oh, I can do that myself," I said. She looked relieved.

I surveyed my purchase, the stamps of 2013, and thought about how countries use postage stamps for propaganda. Stamps present an idealized version of a country and send messages that the country wants to send. This year's haul featured a handful of stamps dedicated to the preservation of biodiversity, problematic in the Philippines. Other stamps featured Filipino film director Gerardo "Gerry" de Leon and the revolutionary Mariano Ponce. As a collector, I covet each of the stamps. Complete coverage gives me psychic satisfaction. Yes, they are political propaganda, but they are also little pieces of art, there to be possessed.

I left the post office and entered a torrential downpour, not a typhoon, but close. I settled in for another wait. I thought about how Joseph had probably found another fare, another person who would listen. Joseph worked six-day weeks, twelve-hour days. He could not escape the constant pressure to earn money to simply survive, nor the perpetually gridlocked Manila traffic, the trash, the problematic utilities, and his low status in a place that worships cash. There are thousands of Josephs and he is one of the lucky ones. He has a job.

Shakey's

"I *like* pizza, Dave. For dinner tonight?" the child asked. Roman loved pizza, as did I.

"We'll have pizza tonight. You can have as much as you want, and it won't matter if you spill. We'll go to a special place," I told the two-year-old.

"Well, birthday boy, you get to choose the restaurant tonight," Marilyn said to me. "Where are we going?"

We were on a family vacation in Boracay with our son, daughter-in-law, and grandson. It was shoulder season, the time between high and low season when only the remnants of passing typhoons can be felt. The winds were cutting and it was starting to rain as we walked along the crowded beach path toward Restaurant Row, making me wonder what the weather might be like in the worst of times. Large plastic panels protected the walkway from the storm coming off the Sea of Mindanao, and people scurried for protection. A metal sign on one of the restaurants was partially dislodged from its hinges, hanging ominously above the crowd.

"Shakey's," I said.

"I know you're kidding. It's about the only chain restaurant in Boracay and the food is terrible. Really, where do you want to go?" Andrew asked.

"Shakey's. No question about it."

"Why would you want to go *there*? It's loud, crowded, and the food is really bad," he said, as if I needed him to tell me again. "Yes, people here like Shakey's—it's a bit like Jollibee. Large servings. Cheap. Lots of sugar."

"I guess I want to go there for the same reason that you don't," I said. "It's time to live a little."

"There's a new Italian place, Caruso's, on our way. You'd like it. Maybe we should go there."

"Andrew, it's your father's birthday. He gets to pick. Shakey's will be okay. Roman will like it," said Kristen.

Andrew, who had lived in Rome for five years, pleaded, "At least *look* at Caruso's. I know people who have been there and I know you'd like it. Great food. Real Italian food. There it is," he said, pointing. "Let's check it out."

We looked in the window and reviewed the menu out front. Yep, selections for each of us. Although nearly empty (it was early), the place was new and trendy looking. It also appeared sanitary.

"You're right," I said, "it looks good. Maybe tomorrow night. Now, it's on to Shakey's."

It was fun to watch Andrew sulk. "I can't believe we've come all the way to Boracay to go there. Doesn't make any sense. Are you sure you wouldn't like Caruso's better? You won't like the pizza at Shakey's. It's too sweet, too much dough."

"Give it up," Kristen said. "Shakey's it is."

"Did you know that Shakey's was cofounded by Sherwood 'Shakey' Johnson, back in the fifties in California?" I said.

"No," Andrew said curtly.

"Sherwood got the nickname 'Shakey' because he shook, due to injuries he sustained in World War II. Once, it was a pretty big chain in the United States, but now it's smaller and many of its outlets are in Asia," I said. "I've seen several in the Philippines."

"Wow, that's interesting," Marilyn said. "I wonder why he named his business after his disability…You know, I'd rather not go to a chain, but since it's your birthday, fair is fair."

"I just want you all to promise you won't mention anything about birthdays to the server. That would be uncomfortable," I said.

Reaching the illuminated Shakey's sign, we entered to the splendor of bright lights, racket, and large servings. We were seated at a wooden picnic table. It was just before six o'clock but the place was packed with families—kids and screaming babies surrounded us, although the table to our left featured a fifty-something American and his teenage Filipina girlfriend. It was noisy, but I liked Shakey's. It seemed to be a real place with local people; despite being a chain, this Filipino-owned franchise felt more like the Philippines than many of the upscale tourist eateries that surrounded the beach. The Greek place, for example, catered to folks from the US, China, Korea, and Japan, not Filipinos.

The harried but friendly waitress took our order: one pizza marinara and one cheese pizza with vegetables. While waiting for our food, Kristen whispered loudly above the clamor that she hoped that I was enjoying my birthday. The waitress noticed. Looking at me, she asked if today was anyone's birthday.

Without thinking, I pointed to two-year-old Roman, saying, "It's *his* birthday!"

"Happy birthday! What is your name?" she asked Roman.

"My name is Roman," he replied.

After the waitress left, I was filled with remorse. How could I lie about my birthday to a two-year-old child? I didn't know why I did it.

My companions didn't let me forget my transgression. Marilyn suggested that there were no bounds to my moral depravity while the others laughed, shaking their heads in what I interpreted as a rebuke.

In truth, the pizza was mediocre, but Roman didn't mind. At his mother's urging, he consumed some of his side salad, but then he entered the land of euphoria. He didn't often have the chance to eat his fill of pizza, but now it was available to him in limitless quantity. He took advantage of the opportunity, devouring more than a child his age really should. The rest of my family was more restrained.

When our meal was finished, an entourage of Shakey's employees surrounded our table and sang "Happy Birthday" to Roman. Startled and intimidated, he put his head down and covered his eyes with his hands as they sang and later congratulated him. Fortunately, they then gave him a large bowl of ice cream with a candle on top.

"Look, Roman," I said. "Ice cream! You're a lucky boy." After a brief hesitation, he dug in, smiling. "Roman," I said, "that looks pretty big. Can I have some?" Roman shared with me.

As we got up to leave, some of the servers returned. "Happy birthday, Roman!" they said, shaking his hand and joking with him. Once outside, Marilyn asked Roman if he knew whose birthday it was.

"Dave's! It's Dave's birthday!" he said with a giggle.

I wasn't sure if Roman understood what had just happened, but I knew that I owed him.

Evening In Ermita

"What would you like to drink?" she said, with a half wink and a smile.

It was the first time I'd ever looked down at a server. She was about three and a half feet tall and her name was Queenie. The large paneled room was dark, except for the glow of the dim lanterns at the bar, scattered candles, and a few small, retro light fixtures. Her little head, rising just beyond the table's edge, had an almost angelic glow to it—it reminded me of sunrise on Siquijor. She was a midget, she said, although she preferred to be called a "little person. Midgets are proportional, just small," she explained. "As long as people keep coming, it doesn't matter what they call me. I'm happy to be a Hobbit."

It was Saturday night and the Hobbit House was packed. A haze of cigarette and cigar smoke permeated the place, and you couldn't hear yourself think—not that you'd want to. When the band started up, things got louder and sweatier, and the stage lights pulsated. It was weird, but it was perfect.

Marilyn was a little put off by the smoke, but she tolerated it for the interesting conversations between sets with the dwarves on staff and the tourists from California at the next table. The band was Remarque, a Filipino act playing American oldies. Schmaltzy, smooth as Grade B Vermont maple syrup—exemplary of its kind. As for the smoke, it was copacetic with me. I probably could have smoked my pipe—no one would have noticed. Unlike Marilyn, I like the smell of smoke.

Marilyn asked for a San Miguel Light, commenting on Queenie's touristy Hobbit House hat, which looked exotic, what with the official seal and logo. They came in many colors, and convenient one-size-fits-all sizing.

"How about a mango shake and a Coke Light?" I said to Queenie, who laughed.

"No beer for you? We have almost two hundred kinds!"

"Maybe later," I said. "Hey, Queenie, we're almost vegetarians. The menu's full of squid, chicken, and sausage. Is there anything that doesn't have meat in it?"

"You know, I'm almost a vegetarian myself. It's healthier. Beer is vegetarian, isn't it? And there's always pizza."

"How *is* your pizza?" Marilyn inquired.

Queenie told us, "Quite frankly, no one comes here for the pizza, but it's passable." We ordered a veggie pizza and hoped for the best.

It might not be a politically correct venue, but the Hobbit House is thriving. We'd first visited it back in 1998, at its previous, smaller location. It's still owned and operated by little people. Except for some of the entertainers and a bartender, the restaurant doesn't hire large folks.

The Hobbit House was founded in 1973 by former Peace Corps volunteer Jim Turner, who, inspired by Tolkien's *Lord of the Rings* trilogy, foresaw a profitable job-creating machine. I found it a droll and whimsical place, more tongue-in-cheek than pathos.

We enjoyed watching the reactions of tourists who stumbled in unaware, who expressed admiration and amusement, pity and confusion. One man seemed to imply that the little people at the Hobbit House were happier and more successful than Filipino dwarves have a right to be. Others were appalled by what they saw as exploitation, the lack of social awareness, and the unabashedly enthusiastic workers. The more capitalistic in the crowd admired the place for turning poverty into a profit center. I suppose folks saw whatever they had come to see.

In the Philippines, it is not unusual to find bars and restaurants with disability themes. For example, the Old West Cowboy Restaurant, in Tagbilaran City, is operated by the deaf—you must communicate through sign language or write your order down. Exploitation? Deaf Filipino cowboys? The food is more than edible, and your purchase helps to educate and provide jobs for impoverished deaf kids in the province of Bohol. It offers baked goods and mango shakes, and it helps to teach the public about deafness. From a local perspective, there is nothing odd about Old West Cowboy.

When we approached the Hobbit House, we encountered a large *Lord of the Rings* mural out front. The faces of the original characters had been cut out and replaced with pictures of the staff. The large, Hobbit-hole entrance had fliers about upcoming entertainment and today's dinner special: deviled sausages. There were also pictures of Munchkins and stories of the lives of little people.

When guests enter, the hostess rings a bell, but tonight no one could possibly have heard the sound. Inside, the walls are filled with framed newspaper clippings from around the world and photos of famous patrons, all praising the Hobbit. Many customers head directly to the best-stocked bar in Manila and ask for pictures with the little people, who seem happy to oblige. We chowed down on the best mediocre pizza we'd ever had while listening to the band. I looked around in the darkness, trying to imagine what the place would look like in the light of day. It was boisterous, and the haze of smoke was rapidly becoming a cloud when I got up to find the restroom, with its low-rise toilet surrounded by Hobbit memorabilia.

I ran into Queenie and asked her how she liked working at the Hobbit. It turned out she was a grandmother, proud to tell me that one of her sons was attending Metro Manila College.

"I *love* it," she said. "It's a great place for a person like me."

"How long have you worked here?"

"Oh, twelve years. The pay is good and the customers are friendly. The people at the bar are locals, at the tables it's usually foreigners. Good tips," she said with a toothful grin. Later, as we finished our pizza, I asked Marilyn what she thought about the place, beyond the smoke.

"Wonderful idea," she said.

"Really? Why do you say that?"

"Look around, David. The employees are enjoying their work, and they seem grateful to be here. I'll bet they make pretty good money, too. Where would they be without this place? It doesn't seem the least bit patronizing."

We watched as a group of Hobbits joined the band in singing "Bad, Bad Leroy Brown." Even the tiny bouncers sang along.

American guidebooks take an overwhelmingly favorable view of the Hobbit House. For example, IExplore.com recently dubbed it as #8 on the list of top dining experiences in the world, and Lonely Planet named it #1 on its list of the most unusual and bizarre bars and restaurants in the world, noting that it's the "world's only bar owned and staffed by Hobbits."

Some foreigners come looking for a freak show. They leave disappointed. The place struck me as a serious bar and restaurant with a theme, great employees, outstanding entertainment, and adequate food. I admired the competence of the management and the psychological gestalt of the workers, who seemed to have their acts together. The vibe said *fun*, not pity. It was a place to be loud, to smoke, to laugh, to enjoy life (and spend money).

Emerging from the smog, like something out of *Casablanca*, Queenie returned to our table, smiling, her image reflected in the glow of my Coke Light can. "Ready for a beer, now?" she said. "Would you like anything else?"

"No, that's it. We would like a box for our leftover pizza."

"How about a T-shirt? A hat?" She carried a stack of each.

I couldn't help myself. I bought a green hat and a blue shirt. I'd be helping the cause, and they're unusual, at least in Lititz, Pennsylvania. "You know," she said, "if you'd have bought five beers you'd get a *free* shirt."

"David, leave a good tip. She's terrific," Marilyn said. "She's bright, competent, and funny. She can give it right back to you."

Queenie returned with our pizza, and we got up, waved goodbye, and headed for the street. I gave her a thumbs up, which she returned.

"Now, the Cowboy Grill," I said.

Marilyn thought it was getting late. "Do you really want to go there?" she asked.

"I promised Stanley I'd go late on a Friday or Saturday night. We're here, we've gotta do it. He said it really gets crazy late at night. It's one of his favorite haunts."

The Cowboy was close, a couple of blocks away, on Mabini Street, although maneuvering through the Saturday night menagerie of panhandlers, drunks, and fun seekers wasn't easy. The area *can* be risky late at night, but no more than places I've frequented in Philadelphia. Call it the price of admission.

You can buy shares of stock in the Cowboy Grill, a subsidiary of Golden Pizza, Inc. The company was founded by Leopoldo L. Prieto back in 1974, the man who brought Shakey's Pizza to the Philippines. For twenty years, the words "Cowboy Grill" have been synonymous with "party time" (and, for some, "crazy time"). It's also a place with strict rules. A sign out front says you must check your weapons at the door, and the Cowboy means business. You're not going to get in with your Uzi or your knife. Or if you're a hooker. The Cowboy doesn't want trouble. It wants you to have fun. It wants your money.

The Cowboy is gigantic and garish, and its exterior reeks of Filipino-style cowboy culture. It hints you'll have fun getting drunk, but in a safe way. It reminded me of Billy Bob's in Fort Worth…big, dark, loud, fun, and commercial. Yes, the neighborhood is a little dangerous, but you don't have to worry: entering the Cowboy Grill is like flying to Tel Aviv. Several menacing-looking, but friendly, armed guards patrol the entrance, and there is even a booth to check your belongings. We approached.

Marilyn had to empty her bag for inspection. She was good to go, except for the cardboard box she was carrying. She opened the box.

"Ah, pizza," one of the guards said, "three slices."

"Do I have to check it?"

"Yes, of course," he said. "Don't worry, we won't eat it."

I had no problems but the guards took a close look at my pipe. They approved.

One of the guards opened the outer doors and we were invited in, a little like entering a vaporous and deafening paradise, only grungier. The lights flashed, the noise was so loud you couldn't tell if a band was performing up front or not, and the air was smoky. The back of the hall is where we'd stay—it was that crowded.

We were escorted to wobbly chairs and a creaky table by a dentally-challenged, anorexic-looking woman with huge breast implants that, unfortunately, strained the credibility of her cowboy getup, complete with red hat and boots. I was afraid she might lose her balance. She'd powdered her face white and slapped on bright red lipstick that just missed the mark. But she was friendly, in a post-lobotomy way, and found us a place to sit in the midst of the craziness of spilled beer, arguments, and laughter. It was tough to tell when you needed to be concerned.

We ordered a couple of beers and looked around. In the distance, up front, we saw a band performing and a crowd of people attempting to dance. Marilyn preferred the acoustic music at the Hobbit House to the hyperamplified noise at the Cowboy.

Closer to us, an eclectic assortment of folks had drunk themselves into varying stages of inebriation. Lots of tourists, locals celebrating birthdays, the occasional lecher, good ole boys, alcoholics, and just regular folks having some fun. In other words, a pretty good cross section of society. People yelled, laughed, and spoke loudly above the din while an army of thin girls maneuvered massive trays of food between the tables. Clearly, servers were chosen for their physiques. The bathrooms were on the other side of the room, and when I edged between the tables, dodging the occasional errant beer, I was greeted like a regular with cries of "Where are you from?" or "Great shirt!" by the cowboys and cowgirls.

It was party time, but we weren't up front as Stanley preferred—we must've been the length of a football field from the stage. Most people were sharing large cylinders filled with beer that probably held a couple gallons each. If only we'd been members of the "Sheriff's Club" we'd have gotten better seats… and better prices.

The hall was filled with hundreds of tables leaving just enough room for a skinny waitress to maneuver her way through without issue. On the perimeter, the assembly-line kitchens served up squid balls and other Filipino specialties, along with fried chicken and beef. This place was making serious money.

We nursed our beers for an hour and didn't enjoy the band. Most of the time we couldn't hear it, and when we could it sounded muffled. We paid our bill at the table and left the Cowboy, waving to our immediate neighbors. Marilyn retrieved her box of pizza from the attendant, still intact. We headed for the curb to hail a cab but were intercepted by a couple of street kids, boys about eight or ten:

"We're hungry…Mister, how about some coins?" the taller

one said.

Marilyn handed them the box of cold pizza and the boys devoured their prize.

Places like the Cowboy Grill and the Hobbit House seem unique to foreign visitors. But the Hobbit has a second restaurant, much smaller, in Boracay, and the Cowboy has expanded to several sites in Metro Manila. It's the commercialization of the unique. Each has a niche, and the openness of the culture encourages innovation.

"You know," I said to Marilyn, "in some ways I can see these places expanding around the world. Of course, I'm not sure you could pull it off in the US."

"You're kidding," she said. "How about Hooters? How about those 'Amish' places? Are we so different?"

Globalization has led to the rapid spread of ideas, especially profitable business ideas. Coupled with economic hardship and dreams of upward mobility, people are often willing to do jobs that might not exist in ordinary times. Most folks do what is necessary to survive, regardless of where they live. Hell, maybe someday we'll have a Hobbit House in Lititz.

Joy

"What would you like, David?" Joy asked. The owner of the Buddha Green chain of restaurants, she was anxious for me to sample the menu and offer an opinion.

"I'll have some of the pork and a little of the chicken," I said, pointing to the buffet at this cafeteria-style restaurant in a working-class neighborhood near Ortigas. The place was similar to small Chinese restaurants found almost everywhere, except for the collection of Buddhas strategically placed around the perimeter. They came in various sizes and shapes, and they were all smiling.

She scooped out my selections and handed the plate to me. I added some rice, green vegetables, and tea and joined her at a table.

I sampled my selections. "This tastes great," I said. "You could've fooled me. What is it?"

Joy was pleased. "The pork is a soy product and the chicken is made from wheat gluten." A slight, kinetic woman, Joy had hunted widely for these ingredients, and she wanted an outsider's opinion. Perhaps the concept of "cheap veggie eats for the masses" could be exported. "Do you have restaurants like this in the US?"

"Not really," I offered. "Where does this stuff come from? It tastes like the real thing. Even the smell and the texture are excellent. I don't think most people could tell the difference. Even pig farmers would think this is pork," I said, hoisting my chopsticks.

"These are from Japan," she said. "They're a little expensive, but the idea of tasty vegetarian fast food will only work if the product is outstanding. The veggie meats need to be healthy and inexpensive, but they must also appeal to customers. People have to be *drawn* here. They have to *want* to eat healthfully, and that is the challenge. Buddha Green is an experiment, both socially and economically. But ultimately it needs to be profitable."

Joy, a Chinoy—a Filipino of Chinese descent (despite her surname, Martinez)—had recently opened the chain, and while this particular restaurant was aimed at the masses, she planned to open an upscale version in one of the big hotels. She was also toying with the idea of expanding to other countries in Southeast Asia.

Buddha Green restaurants are new here, but Joy liked to think big. Once established in a neighborhood, they grow, but slowly at first. Most folks aren't used to the concept of vegetarian food—it sounds foreign to them, and not particularly appetizing. Joy wanted to lure people into veggie-land, but it had to taste good, or it would be once-and-done.

"You know, David," she said, "Filipinos are addicted to sweetened foods that aren't good for them. The obesity rate is high here, and diabetes is epidemic. The people are not healthy. They suffer because the food they can afford makes them lethargic, overweight, and sick. The Philippines could have a bright future if people would reform. I'd like to do something about the poor health of the people," she said with a smile, "but trying to change an entrenched culture is difficult." Joy lived up to her name.

"I've noticed that sugar is added to almost everything here. Even bread. I love the fresh fruit, but not the local food. Too much fried meat and sweets," I said, "although I must confess I love *ube* ice cream."

"You see," she said, "Mr. Donut, Dunkin' Donuts, Magnolia, and Auntie Anne's are popular here because the people are addicted to sugar. We can't advance as a society until we change this. I'm hoping that Buddha Green will show people that it is possible to eat tasty, inexpensive, and healthy food all at once… I'm not doing this for the money—I have money."

"It's funny," I said, "Auntie Anne's is headquartered a few miles from my house, and the others are mostly American companies. What have we done?"

"You can't simply blame the Americans—Filipinos are a receptive audience, and most of the franchises are Filipino owned. After World War II, companies set up shop here, corporations from all over the world. The Americans were the most successful, because Filipinos wanted to be like Americans. They still do," she said. "Americans sell what people want and can afford."

Joy, a divorced, fifty-something woman, enjoyed great wealth despite her middle-class origins—her former husband was one of the richest men in the country. She was also a devout Buddhist, a vegetarian, an excellent palm reader, and more than a little secretive. She was tough to find, with good reason. Wealthy people like herself are targeted by kidnappers, and she was careful, very careful. Joy traveled in a Land Cruiser with blacked-out windows in the company of two large, austere gentlemen in business suits. I had dinner with her several times, and in each instance I was told to go to a specific location near my hotel, where I'd be picked up by her car and informed where we were eating. She never had dinner at the same place two nights in a row, and her "assistants" were always discreetly nearby. Earlier that evening we'd dined at the Manila Hotel in a private room. It was a difficult way for her to live, but a realistic adaptation to the realities she faced. Usually smiling, she often laughed, and looked for the potential for good in bad situations, liberally quoting the Buddha.

I'd met Joy through a friend of mine, an official with the Humane Society of the United States in Washington, DC. He said Joy had called him about problems she was having with her neighbors stemming from the number of cats she had in her home—she hadn't made any progress with Filipino organizations. He knew I was going to Manila and asked me to look in on her.

Joy took me to her home in an affluent enclave near Valle Verde. It was a large residence, but not opulent, and I immediately noticed the security, consisting of several strategically placed guards and cameras. What made the house unusual was a large addition, a combination of hospital and sanctuary for stray cats. Inside were a couple of hundred felines, with room to play, a number of attendants, and a veterinarian who checked in regularly. These were the lucky ones, salvaged from the thousands of street cats found around the city. Their new home was clean and built for feline comfort, despite the relative crowding. From the outside, I didn't notice any cat odor (I'm an expert on the subject), and only the occasional quiet meow. It was a high-quality warehouse.

"Many people disregard the animals," she said, "although we know that they're sentient beings who have individual personalities just like humans. They have as much of a right to live as we do. I'm trying to save as many as I can, but I'm running out of room. I'd like to get as many cats adopted as possible. It's been difficult, and some of my neighbors have not been supportive. Right now things are calm. I've tried to teach them about the cats…"

I suggested she form an organization of like-minded people to help protect the cats and get them adopted. She couldn't do it by herself, and I provided some models for how such a group could work and methods she might use to find others interested in the cause. I realized that she needed to balance her need for personal safety with her desire to help. Surely there were a few neighbors who, once they understood, would assist her. I told her there were others concerned about the cats and that I'd encountered a number of small informal groups, often foreign professionals, who cared for neighborhood cats. Unfortunately, they were found largely in affluent areas of town. The major hurdle she faced was that human life was cheap in the Philippines, and animal life cheaper still. Until that changed, the cat problem would be difficult to address. She understood the challenges, but was undeterred—a happy warrior.

Joy was an unusual person in that she was using her wealth to improve the lot of both people and animals. She understood that she would need to build an organization that would outlive her, and she knew that her successors would require that Buddha Green be profitable for it to survive. She was investing her money in human and animal progress, and she had a timeline—she wasn't immortal. I was impressed with how she, a woman alone in the impoverished and polluted city of Manila, cheerfully tackled some of the most intractable problems in her world. I was also encouraged that she readily acknowledged her mortality and was taking steps while still relatively young and healthy to improve the world around her, in a way that would continue even after her demise. Perhaps she'd be rewarded for her efforts in her next life.

Epilogue

June 14, 2014

My friend Stanley is in Cebu on vacation, and this morning he posted a comment on Facebook: "In my last two days here in Cebu, Philippines, I have seen terrible sights that I would never wish on anyone. Little kids, very small, laid out sleeping on a busy pavement, people stepping over them. Not a blanket or anything on them, with a mother close by holding *two* young babies in her arms. She was sleeping on the pavement as many, many people walked by. I am so sorry to say I walked by with my friend Arturo, and I thought of my sons, my grandchildren. As I have many times on this long trip, I thought about how thankful I am to live in the United States." Later, with perhaps a twinge of remorse, he added, "I'm going to the grocery store to buy some food for them."

What he describes is not unusual in Cebu, nor in most of the Philippines. Almost immediately he received a reply from one of his Facebook friends, a Filipina: "No, Mr. Stanley. Not everyone is in poverty in our country. There are some listed in the World's Richest. There are many enjoying the life of the rich and famous. Mr. Stanley, you are describing the poorest level of our society, which every country has."

Alternate realities? Or does this sound familiar? If you live at the Rockwell, you might think wealth is the norm and that poverty is an aberration. Intellectually, you know that you are in a fortunate minority, but on a day-to-day basis the mores and customs of where you live shape your view of the world. What you experience daily forms your view of what is "normal" and finally "acceptable." It is your frame of reference and the prism through which you see the world.

If you travel widely in the Philippines, perhaps you develop a Filipino viewpoint. When Americans first come to the Philippines, they tend to look at the place from the point of view of American culture and are sometimes quick to make judgments based on preconceptions, not realizing that what they see might not be "the way things are." Other folks arrive with global perspectives, a global outlook. These people have not simply lived in different countries, but they've absorbed cultural differences *within* those countries. After traveling extensively, I am not as quick to make judgments about new people and places, and have tried, often unsuccessfully, to understand the cultural context of a new place, to begin to see just below the surface. But I'm an American, subject to the blind spots and prejudices that our culture fosters, and I too often tend to reject new information that is at odds with my view of reality.

I try not to judge people or their motives, knowing that they, too, have their own preconceptions, blind spots, and truth. I don't blame Joseph for giving me the hard sell to buy a condo; if I were in his position, I'd probably do the same. I understand why Augusta prefers the splendid isolation of the Rockwell and why so many want to believe in Roman.

I'm not without opinions, however. Travel has given me a perspective that I wouldn't otherwise have. I've seen the beaches in New Jersey, Phuket, Bohol, the Caribbean, and elsewhere, and can draw some comparisons, offer some opinions. Comparing beaches is easier than comparing the judgments of people in their unique environments. As far as I know, I'll have only one life on this planet, and I'd like to understand and experience this place. I have another motive: one key to healthy longevity is having an insatiable appetite for the new, the unusual. You might call it an addiction—this time, a *positive* one.

In this collection of essays, I've tried to depict a little of the diversity and complexity of Filipino culture. Why *isn't* Tony in jail? There are placards in airports, at hotels, beaches, and elsewhere urging visitors to report sex trafficking—yet it flourishes. There are many facets to the modern Philippines; my goal has been to present a few of them, in at least some of their complexity.

I'm comfortable in the Philippines. It's not quite home, but it is familiar, excitingly soothing. While I'll never understand the culture like a native, I've seen changes over the past twenty years, and I have formed some opinions about what I've seen, what I see. The Philippines is a flawed paradise, but still a paradise. Many of the country's islands are almost untouched, with superb beaches, pristine waters, and biodiversity that is almost unimaginable to an American. Until recently, most foreigners have seen the Philippines as a place of unrelenting natural disasters. They read about typhoons, mudslides, earthquakes, erupting volcanoes, ferry sinkings, and troubles in the south with Muslim separatists, and they avoid travel there. American tour promoters tend to omit the country. I noticed, for example, that *National Geographic Explorations 2014–2015*, which sells tours to countries around the world, overlooks the Philippines completely, although they'll gladly take you to Vietnam or Cambodia.

Foreigners are just beginning to read about places like Boracay, Bohol, and Palawan, which are rapidly becoming a Beulah Land for tourists, but they avoid the rest of the country outside of Manila. This is a mistake, because the unknown parts of the country are largely safe, noncommercial, inexpensive, and often striking.

When you arrive at Manila's Aquino Airport, you arrive

at a modern, Westernized facility. Superficially, it feels almost American. As you leave you encounter the chaos found at airports in most parts of the world, with first-time visitors trying to figure out how to navigate the way downtown. On the cab trip to your hotel you realize that you are in a complex land of both excruciating poverty and hypercapitalistic development. On the road heading into the city you observe a seemingly endless collection of gigantic billboards touting the new casinos, upscale residential developments, and the latest fashions. In the distance you contemplate an armada of skyscrapers under construction.

Exiting the main highway, you encounter something different in the neighborhoods you pass. Extensive jerry-built slums embrace the visitor, flimsy structures awaiting the next typhoon, the next round of death. If you observe your surroundings closely, you might see a naked man rummaging through an overflowing trash can, a man beating a woman with a stick, or a couple of men casually urinating against a wall while an old woman dressed in rags nonchalantly eats her orange cream popsicle nearby. You see people sleeping under highway overpasses, in the mausoleums in the Chinese cemetery, and in purloined shopping carts in Ermita.

What the visitor cannot see is the social fabric of the slums, a world in which more cooperation exists than you might imagine. In such an interconnected place, there are people who can fix a bicycle…or your collapsing ceiling. There are supportive families, and a couple of people have fax machines. You can get what you need here. People help each other. They need to if they're to survive, and family ties are the only safety net for most folks. They have nothing, but they get by. What else can they do?

Checking into a place like the Pan Pacific Hotel, you are again back in first-world comfort, ready to explore the grotesque beauty of the city. The fiery sunset over Manila Bay is embellished by pollution, and the bay has served as a waste bin for the city's millions for generations. On my first trip to Manila in the mid-1990s, the bay was a sea of floating debris, with kids swimming among the flotsam looking for anything of value, perhaps a bottle to recycle or a discarded toy to take home. Or maybe to just cool off. Surrounding the water was a decaying concrete wall. Trash was strewn liberally everywhere you looked.

But change has come to Manila Bay, not only with the advent of new hotels and office buildings, but with the increasing cleanliness of the area. Signs remind folks to place trash in the receptacles, and most people comply. Rojas Avenue, the main highway parallel to the bay, is now an attractive boulevard, with a new bay walk, modern lighting, new retaining walls, and sidewalks. It looks clean and modern, despite the trash that still sometimes appears in the water. The bay isn't what it could be, but it is significantly better than it was.

I've seen the country gradually improve. Environmental protection and awareness have escalated, albeit slowly. When you go to a developed tourist spot like Boracay, you'll notice beach regulations are as vigorously enforced as in the United States. There are lots of rules, and they are observed. Increasingly, the national government has awakened to the opportunities. With the right publicity, perhaps those Americans who spend thousands of dollars vacationing in places like the Jersey Shore and Florida might be enticed to come to the Philippines. Or at least those world travelers who might otherwise head for places like Thailand or Taiwan.

Filipinos are proud of their country's natural beauty, often inquiring if I have been here or there, eager to describe their favorite place, which is often their home province. Filipinos are gradually learning the role of the citizen in protecting their world. This mentality needs to be fostered if ecotourism is to succeed. Filipinos need to have a vested interest in their country.

The nation is fast becoming a service economy, bolstered by remittances from abroad. Girls placed by Tony send money home, as do all-arounders like Rosa and servers at places like

Shakey's or Starbucks. This enables families to survive. Call centers employ many thousands of people, enabling them to escape abject poverty. Companies like Intel and Sketchers offer manufacturing jobs. There is a tourist market for Filipinos who now live abroad as permanent residents. "Heritage" tours are gaining traction.

The Philippines is on the cusp of developing a global ecotourist enterprise along the lines of much smaller Costa Rica. There will be hyperexploitation, beyond anything we've seen thus far in Palawan, or even Boracay. It will attract hotels, restaurants, malls, all the accoutrements of a tourist-oriented economy. There is money to be made.

This shift will create new wealth, much of which will accrue to the existing oligarchy, which will finance the expansion. Many jobs will be created, which will improve the lives of the general population. Young girls will be able to stay at home and work at a hotel or in a mall rather than apply to Tony for placement, and boys will find jobs in their local towns, rather than abroad. Maybe Jo-Jo will find a better job locally, so she won't have to leave her child with her sister and move to Hong Kong.

We might look at these low-wage jobs as simple American-style exploitation, but, in truth, they are a salvation for many people, many families, especially the young. After all, resorts need to be built, erected by people who will happily work for a few dollars a day. Is this "trickle-down" economics, or is it "bottom-up?" Perhaps it is both.

Signs of change are pervasive. For example, the village of Ternate, a town that traditionally subsisted on fishing, has seen its fish catch decline precipitously over the past decade. But with highway, mall, and housing developments, new opportunities for employment in the area have emerged. The girls in the village no longer need to sit at the market all day hoping to sell a few fish. Sales clerks are needed, and there are hotel rooms to clean, front desks to man, the first rung on the ladder.

I cannot explain why I am drawn here, to a land with so many extremes. Perhaps it's because I have never seen a place so overpowering in its vividness, its intensity. Bright colors are accentuated by the strong fragrances of kinetic life, a place where cities are as frenetic as the backcountry is placid and untouched in the tropical sun. People are friendly and inquisitive, happy, yet stoic: they ask you how much money you make and want to know where you come from. They usually make assumptions about you. You must be rich, because you have traveled far. Surely you have domestic help. They can't conceive of middle-class America any more than we can comprehend what it might be like to be a pineapple picker in Mindanao.

The Philippines is home to all manner of recurring tragedy, constant reminders of the fragility of the place, of how difficult it can be to survive here. Make no mistake: living in the Philippines, for most people, is a daily struggle. There are now one hundred million Filipinos, though the rate of population growth has fallen to a still unsustainable 2 percent. The fertility rate has fallen to just over three children per family, high but an improvement. Life expectancy is surprisingly good at sixty-nine for men and seventy-five for women. Still, in a country with an excessive birthrate and with only 4 percent of the population over the age of sixty-five (more than one-third are under fifteen), the need for jobs and education, for housing and infrastructure, is pressing. Given the depth of the privation here, *any* job helps. Can development, planning, and technology outpace demographics?

Perhaps what seduces the visitor is the uniqueness of the culture: a blend of Malaysian, Indonesian, Indian, and Chinese overlaid with centuries of domination by the Spanish, followed by the Americans and the Japanese, ending with homegrown suppression by dictators like Ferdinand and Imelda Marcos and thugs like Joseph "Erap" Estrada. Subjugated for centuries, Filipinos have developed a culture of amalgamation, able to synthesize the new and different into what is old and established. They have learned to be adaptable, flexible, and tolerant. But there is a dark side to these traits, the acceptance of the intolerable, of street kids in paradise. Many Filipinos exhibit a willingness to do whatever it takes to find a modicum of success, whether it is Tony trafficking in young girls, Lemon's work as an all-arounder, or the many who enter prostitution. Psychologically, some have given up. For them, things will never change. They simply endure.

I doubt there will be a revolution in the Philippines, at least not an armed one, however desirable that might be. Even in this kleptocracy, the velocity of change in a shrinking world can overwhelm. There is a middle class and it is growing. International corporations are entering the country at an unprecedented rate, and they are beginning to demand reform. Multinational enterprises do not like controversy and scandal. They simply want to sell products and make money. They can be a positive force for change.

I'm conflicted about the future of the country. What if jobs and infrastructure don't keep pace with population growth? What happens if foreign remittances decline? Will there be political reform? Even the most corrupt presidential candidate campaigns on a platform of reducing crime in high places, only to subsequently be indicted. For example, President Gloria Macapagal Arroyo gave her predecessor Joseph Estrada "executive clemency," but was later herself arrested for corruption. And there are powerful vested interests that mitigate against seismic change. The handful of extended families who own the country will not relinquish power easily—it is simply more expeditious, at least until recently, to pay higher fees to control the politicians. The rich are growing richer and the concentration of wealth dwarfs that of the United States. It's almost a parody. The corruption and disparity of wealth are more obvious. It's as if a US-style government were carried to its logical conclusion, complete with gated communities, kidnapping, and not even the pretense of "government by the people." Filipinos don't trust their government, and for good reason.

In a nation whose major export is its youth, remittances from overseas workers is an industry that folks will not want to risk giving up. While cash transfers from these workers increase yearly, the number of workers is not growing as fast as it had been. Still, the *Manila Bulletin* contains daily lists of international jobs that entice young people to leave. Bakers, baristas, and cashiers are needed in Dubai, and ya-yas in places like Canada and Australia. Electricians are needed in Saudi Arabia, as are painters and plumbers, and all manner of skilled tradesmen. If you are a decent refrigeration technician or a nurse, you can earn good money abroad. Even if you are simply a laborer, there is a job for you somewhere, a place that pays more than you're making now.

The Philippines presents a warning for Americans. When family corporations and crony capitalists control government, when wealth is concentrated in the extreme, and when exploitation becomes a sport, the society is stunted, filled with wasted lives, wasted talent. Crime, corruption, and poverty combine to create a citizenry where only some can strive and advance. For others, the desperation is palpable. You feel it in a taxi with Joseph or in all-arounders like Lemon. You see it in the family of Nang Conching.

While most simply accept things as they are and try to enjoy life in paradise, others struggle against the odds to improve their situations and are sometimes successful—Philippine Women's University is filled with such stories. With development, there will be more jobs where people live, perhaps mitigating the need for dispatching one's daughter to Cebu or Manila, one's son to Rome. In the interim, why obey the law? It's a fool's game. If you pay taxes, the government will steal your money. Better to cut a deal with your local tax collector.

I once spoke with a small-town tax collector who lived in a home built mostly of marble, courtesy of the Marcos regime. "Why should I send the taxes I collect to Manila? Those crooks will just keep the money for themselves. It's better to let the people have the money. It's better to give people a break, be flexible."

"With a little for you?" I asked.

"Well, of course. I have to live, too!"

The Philippines will continue to export workers, although the rate is apt to slow with the rising economy. The country has an opportunity to transform itself, to be a world-class destination, while preserving its natural charms. This will require changes in governance. A culture of bribery, extortion, and money laundering will inhibit these changes. Progress will require systemic change, and this change will have to be led by the wealthy, who are beginning to view it as in their own self-interest. Many of the country's "high ones" want a level playing field in commerce, free of the service charges they now incur, free of worrying about the selective enforcement of the law, or kidnapping. Many would prefer to simply pay more in taxes and get on with their business. Some see the writing on the wall that overt kleptocracy is not sustainable.

Economic change is unfolding before our eyes. Will political evolution follow? Recent trends suggest that progress is being made, with the *Manila Bulletin* and the *Philippine Inquirer* featuring daily exposés of corrupt politicians. The emerging middle class is beginning to agitate for change, and some of the wealthy are growing weary of the present system. Eventually, the Philippines will become more democratic. It will be a Filipino version of representative government that is apt to recognize the power of the Catholic Church and be respectful of the oligopoly that controls the economic life of the country.

Perhaps we will see in the Philippines a movement toward

American-style politics, governed by money and connections, but more transparent and open to anyone with sufficient resources to play the game. Ironically, one might argue that the United States is moving toward more invasive, less open government, controlled by an oligopoly. Are the Bush and Clinton dynasties really so different from the Aquinos? The Arroyos?

Until the new Philippines emerges, the fatalistically optimistic Filipino people will persevere as they always have. Perhaps all-arounder Rosa put it best: "I am very surviving."

About The Author

David Brubaker is happiest when exploring and traveling, mindful that there is much to see and time marches on. He has worked and studied in a wide variety of countries, most notably the Philippines and China. He especially enjoys visiting neighborhoods, interacting with local residents, and has an eye for the unusual. He lives in Lititz, Pennsylvania with his wife Marilyn and their three cats.

Also by ThingsAsian Press

Light and Silence
Growing Up in My Mother's Alaska

By Janet Brown
Photographs from the author's private collection
2015, 5 1/2 x 8 1/2 inches; 144 pages; paperback; color & b/w images
ISBN: 978-1-934159-56-9
$12.95

Almost Home
The Asian Search of a Geographic Trollop

By Janet Brown
Photographs by Janet Brown
2013, 5 1/2 x 8 1/2 inches; 210 pages; paperback; color images
ISBN: 978-1-934159-55-2
$12.95

Defiled on the Ayeyarwaddy

By Ma Thanegi
Photographs by Ma Thanegi
2010, 5 1/2 x 8 1/2 inches; 256 pages; paperback; color images
ISBN: 978-1-934159-24-8
$12.95

Nor Iron Bars a Cage

By Ma Thanegi
2013, 5 1/2 x 8 1/2 inches; 176 pages; paperback
ISBN: 978-1-934159-50-7
$12.95

Tone Deaf in Bangkok
(and other places)

By Janet Brown
Photographs by Nana Chen
2009, 5 1/2 x 8 1/2 inches; 160 pages; paperback; color images
ISBN: 978-1-934159-12-5
$12.95

Vignettes of Taiwan
Short Stories, Essays & Random Meditations About Taiwan

By Joshua Samuel Brown
2006, 5 1/2 x 8 1/2 inches; 160 pages; paperback; color images
ISBN: 978-0-971594-08-1
$12.95

Eternal Harvest
The Legacy of American Bombs in Laos

By Karen J. Coates
Photographs by Jerry Redfern
2013, 5 1/2 x 8 1/2 inches; 380 pages; paperback; 218 images
ISBN: 978-1-934159-49-1
$12.95

This Way More Better
Stories and Photos from Asia's Back Roads

By Karen J. Coates
Photographs by Jerry Redfern
2013, 5 1/2 x 8 1/2 inches; 288 pages; paperback; color images
ISBN: 978-1-934159-48-4
$12.95

Vignettes of Japan

By Celeste Heiter
Photographs by Robert George
2003, 5 1/2 x 8 1/2 inches; 180 pages; paperback; color images
ISBN: 978-0-971594-02-9
$12.95

Taiwan Tattoo

By Brian M. Day
2015, 5 1/2 x 8 1/2 inches; 216 pages; paperback
ISBN: 978-1-934159-64-4
$12.95

ThingsAsian Press

Experience Asia Through the Eyes of Travelers

"To know the road ahead, ask those coming back."
(Chinese proverb)

East meets West at ThingsAsian Press, where the secrets of Asia are revealed by the travelers who know them best. Writers who have lived and worked in Asia. Writers with stories to tell about basking on the beaches of Thailand, teaching English conversation in the exclusive salons of Tokyo, trekking in Bhutan, haggling with antique vendors in the back alleys of Shanghai, eating spicy noodles on the streets of Jakarta, photographing the children of Nepal, cycling the length of Vietnam's Highway One, traveling through Laos on the mighty Mekong, and falling in love on the island of Kyushu.

Inspired by the many expert, adventurous and independent contributors who helped us build **ThingsAsian.com**, our publications are intended for both active travelers and those who journey vicariously, on the wings of words.

ThingsAsian Press specializes in travel stories, photo journals, cultural anthologies, destination guides and children's books. We are dedicated to assisting readers in exploring the cultures of Asia through the eyes of experienced travelers.

www.thingsasianpress.com